D1190369

Without Justification

Without Justification

Jonathan Sutton

A Bradford Book
The MIT Press
Cambridge, Massachusetts
London, England

© 2007 Massachusetts Institute of Technology

All rights reserved. No part of this book may be reproduced in any form by any electronic or mechanical means (including photocopying, recording, or information storage and retrieval) without permission in writing from the publisher.

MIT Press books may be purchased at special quantity discounts for business or sales promotional use. For information, please email special_sales@mitpress.mit.edu or write to Special Sales Department, The MIT Press, 55 Hayward Street, Cambridge, MA 02142.

This book was set in Stone and Stone Sans by Windfall Software using ZzTEX, and was printed and bound in the United States of America.

Library of Congress Cataloging-in-Publication Data

Sutton, Jonathan, 1951–
Without justification / by Jonathan Sutton
    p. cm.
"A Bradford Book."
Includes bibliographical references and index.
ISBN-13: 978-0-262-19555-3 (hc : alk. paper)
ISBN-10: 0-262-19555-0 (hc : alk. paper)
ISBN-13: 978-0-262-69347-9 (pbk. : alk. paper)
ISBN-10: 0-262-69347-X (pbk. : alk. paper)
1. Justiciation (Theory of knowledge). 2. Knowledge, Theory of. I. Title.
BD212.S88   2006
121'.4—dc22

2006046671

10 9 8 7 6 5 4 3 2 1

Contents

Preface

Much of this book is probably worthless—ill considered, if not false. But most of it is not. (We will return to the matter of the preface—and how to avoid paradox as I hope to have done above—in section 2.4.) For that happy state of affairs, I am indebted to my colleagues at Southern Methodist University—Doug Ehring, Eric Barnes, David Hausman, Steve Sverdlik, and, especially, Mark Heller and Robert Howell. Thanks for contributions, philosophical and otherwise, are also due to Leila Batarseh, Mark McCullagh, Ram Neta, Timothy Williamson, James Penner, Mike Thau, Eric Margolis, Daniel McLean, Mark Sainsbury, and, above all, to Dana Nelkin, without whose work this book might well never have existed.

Philosophers often do well to pay attention to the philosophically highly unorthodox yet commonplace and reasonable assumptions made by those outside the professional philosophical community. For making me aware of just such an assumption (the endorsement of which is, fundamentally, the first half of this book), I am very grateful to John Lilly, Dara Salem, and Dianna Schmitz.

Introduction

Justified belief has been the subject of contentious debate among episte-mologists for quite some time. Can a believer tell "from the inside," by in-trospection alone, whether a belief is justified or unjustified (is justification internalist)? Or can somewhat inaccessible facts about the believer's exter-nal environment make or break justified belief (is justification externalist)? Is justification perhaps located between those two poles, partially internal-ist and partially externalist? What has justification to do with knowledge? Is justification a *component* of knowledge? If so, what else is required for a belief to constitute knowledge? Most agree that Gettier showed that truth alone is not sufficient to render a justified belief knowledge (Gettier 1963). And if justification is not a component of knowledge, what exactly is the relation between justification and knowledge? Should justification be aban-doned in favor of the notion of warrant, which by definition combines with truth to yield knowledge?

Even if we confined our attention exclusively to either the internalist or externalist camp, we should find plenty of disagreement. Despite the many differences among epistemologists and philosophers in general concerning justification, there is consensus on one point. Whatever justification is, and whatever its relation to knowledge, justification—if it exists at all— is distinct from knowledge. In particular, there are justified beliefs that do not amount to knowledge, even if all instances of knowledge are instances of justified belief.

This work opposes that consensus. Justified belief simply is knowledge, and not because there is a lot more knowledge than has been supposed, but because there are a lot fewer justified beliefs. There are, for example, no false justified beliefs.

The consensus I speak of is a consensus among *contemporary* epistemologists. The claim that the only worthwhile beliefs in any important *epistemic* sense—the only worthwhile beliefs so far as *rationality* goes—are those that amount to knowledge is paid little attention by philosophers of the recent past. The *negation* of that claim would, I suggest, have been considered unworthy of consideration by many previous generations of philosophers, from the Socrates of Plato's *Apology* onward. Drawing a distinction between justified belief and knowledge—a distinction that is supposed to correspond to a difference in the *extension* of the two concepts—is a practice of rather recent vintage. And I will be arguing that the practice is ill founded.

(Many philosophers of the past stressed that knowledge consists of beliefs for which the believer has good reasons—the basis, in large part, for the common claim that knowledge was traditionally defined as justified, true belief. However, it is not at all clear that such philosophers took themselves to have an understanding of the notion of *good* reasons that was independent of, and conceptually prior to, their understanding of the notion of knowledge itself. If they intended their remarks as a *definition,* they would have to have taken themselves to have such an understanding. It is quite possible that most such philosophers took the goodness of reasons to consist in their sufficing for knowledge of what they were reasons for [and hence as *entailing* the truth of the belief for which they were reasons].)

My view clearly falls within Timothy Williamson's (2000) nascent discipline of knowledge-centered epistemology. For Williamson, we should not practice epistemology by aiming to understand knowledge in terms of allegedly more fundamental epistemic concepts. Rather, we should aim to understand epistemic phenomena in terms of the concept of knowledge, taking that to be the most fundamental epistemic concept. Although this work is not consistent with Williamson's stated views on various epistemic matters taken as a whole since he does from time to time employ a concept of justification that is supposed to be distinct from knowledge, it is not *wildly* inconsistent with them, as it is with most other epistemology. I engage more with Williamson's views on various subjects than with those of any other epistemologist throughout the book and build upon them in a number of places. Nevertheless, the questions that I address are, by and large, distinct from those that Williamson has addressed.

Williamson's slogan is "Knowledge First." Perhaps mine should be "Knowledge First *and Last*." I aim to show, first, that we do not and maybe cannot have a serviceable notion of justification that is distinct from knowledge, and, second, that we do not need one—we can get by better in epistemology without one. To this end, I explore a couple of key epistemological topics—testimony and inference—aiming to give an entirely satisfactory account of those topics that relies on the notion of knowledge alone. We must get by in epistemology without justification conceived of as something distinct from knowledge and are better off without justification. Justification is often used in various philosophical debates to glue together beliefs into a single category which encompasses both instances of knowledge and instances of *mere* (allegedly) justified belief. Such tactics amount to gerrymandering if my view is correct, and we need to abandon them; I show how to do so in two central cases.

The first chapter explains what the view is in detail by distinguishing four notions of justification that I identify with knowledge from some less important notions (such as blameless belief, the grounds for its blamelessness not being purely epistemic) that one calls 'justification' only at the peril of conflating quite distinct phenomena. The chapter starts by laying out intuitive cases of justified belief that do not constitute knowledge; the work of undermining those intuitions is partially complete by the end of the chapter.

The second chapter starts by giving four independent arguments for the view that justification is knowledge. Undermining the intuitions that speak in favor of distinguishing justification from knowledge is at least as important as my positive arguments, and I complete the bulk of that work after giving my arguments and discussing some objections to them. I argue that there is much confusion in epistemology because 'justified belief that *p*' has often been used indiscriminately to denote both justified belief that *p* and justified belief that *probably p*. Such a loose use of the phrase 'justified belief' is entirely serviceable outside philosophy (and sometimes within), but epistemology done right demands strict maintenance of the distinction. I illustrate this by discussing the lottery paradox (once more, since it is the basis of one of my earlier arguments) and the paradox of the preface. I continue the chapter by arguing that knowledge is not mysterious even if it is not definable in a traditional manner since we can be functionalists about knowledge, which legitimates a somewhat promiscuous use of competing traditional definitions of knowledge. It does not legitimate contextualism, one of the few broad approaches to knowledge that I do not draw from in the following chapter—just as well since I close the chapter by arguing that it is false. (Just under half of the material in the first two chapters appears in my paper "Stick to What You Know," appearing in *Noûs*, September 2005, 39:3 pp. 359–396.)

The third chapter argues for a view of testimony that has received nothing but scant dismissal in the literature—one can know that *p* by testimony only if one knows that he who testifies that *p* knows that *p*. This is not a consequence of the view of justification defended in the previous two chapters. My argument requires substantial independent premises (the falsity of all tenable less stringent views) in addition to the claim that justification is knowledge, and I argue for those premises. I also argue for "the KK view" without *any* reliance on the claim that justification is knowledge. In parallel, I explore how one should conceive of justified testimonial belief if one *does* distinguish justification and knowledge, arguing that a very stringent view of justified testimonial belief would also be called for. The stringency of the KK view (and the allied view concerning (alleged) justification) has been overestimated, leading, I suggest, to its lack of partisans. Although the KK view grants testimonial knowledge only when quite high epistemic standards have been met, those standards can be and are met regularly by normal human beings (even children, perhaps)—or so I argue.

The final chapter concerns inference. Unlike the previous chapter, the chapter draws (apparently alarming) consequences of my view that justification is knowledge and argues that they are actually *beneficial* consequences that add support to my view. In one important sense of 'inference', a "good" inference leads to a conclusion belief in which is justified. So an inference cannot be good unless it leads to knowledge of the conclusion. I argue that this consequence of my view is not unwelcome, and, at least when it comes to the question of when one has evidence *for* a hypothesis, itself has quite welcome consequences: it leads to a simple and compelling account of evidence. As with the phrase 'justified belief', the phrase 'evidence that *h*' is used indiscriminately to denote both evidence that *h* and evidence that *probably h*—and sometimes even evidence that there is at least a small chance that *h*, depending upon the circumstances in which the assertion of evidence is made. We should, however, distinguish these phenomena even if *no* existing sense of 'evidence' does so, and we need to introduce a new sense of the word in terms of which more standard uses of the term can be defined. Evidence for a hypothesis in the strict (and possibly novel) sense enables one who has that evidence to know the hypothesis. Problem cases surrounding the notion of evidence are susceptible to coherent and satisfying treatment if we define the "evidence-for" relation thus. Preparatory to my discussion of evidence, I consider whether knowledge is closed under known logical implication ("closure"), arguing that it is not and that that is not surprising or alarming if justification is knowledge. I also discuss inductive inference in general, apart from the notion of evidence.

Almost all epistemology is heavily shaped by consideration of philosophical skepticism since almost all epistemology operates under the constraint that we know a good deal of what we commonly take ourselves to know and operates with some more or less developed conception (or conceptions) of knowledge that makes quotidian knowledge possible. This work is no exception. However, I devote almost no explicit attention to the matter of philosophical skepticism itself and hope to demonstrate by example that this is a quite feasible way of doing epistemology (not that I am the first to proceed in this manner).

On the other hand, in two respects, this work *promotes* skepticism of a nonphilosophical variety. It promotes skepticism about a large chunk of philosophy itself. People have taken the notion of justification as something distinct from knowledge quite seriously for quite some time. I argue that there is nothing to the notion. Further, I propose that a good deal of the attraction that justification has is based on a failure to use *words* strictly (shudder), which to many will seem an embarrassing regression to the dark days of analytic philosophy. I, of course, hope that the burden of embarrassment will fall on others' shoulders!

Second, I argue that *everyone*, philosopher and nonphilosopher alike, should stick to what they know—one should only believe something if one knows it to be so. Further, one should not believe what someone tells one unless one knows that he knows what he is talking about. Everyone thinks that many beliefs are unjustified, but there are a lot more unjustified beliefs on my view than for perhaps anyone but a philosophical skeptic since many beliefs indeed fail to conform to those two standards. (Although not as many as there might appear, I argue in the second chapter.) Perhaps, then, I am the next worst thing to a philosophical skeptic. Readers might wonder if I really believe the views defended here. I assure them that I do. That, it should be clear by now, is a very strong commitment indeed. (I believe that the *details* merely have an even chance of being correct.)

1   The View

1.1   Introduction

My view is that a subject's belief that *p* is justified if and only if he knows that *p:* justification *is* knowledge. I will start by describing two broad classes of allegedly justified beliefs that do not constitute knowledge and which hence cannot be what they are often taken to be if my view is correct. It is far from clear what my view is until I say a lot more about the relevant concept or concepts of justification that concern me. The following section describes several concepts of justification that epistemologists have employed and, in particular, identifies four concepts of justification that I claim are coextensive with the concept of knowledge. One of those is the deontological conception of justification: my view is that one ought not believe that *p* unless one knows that *p*. I imagine that the major opposition to my view will be that it is simply *obvious* that there are justified false beliefs, a feeling that I try to dispel in the lengthy section on concepts of justification before I finally get around to giving the main arguments in favor of my view in the next chapter. Indeed, undermining the intuitive support for the claim that there are justified beliefs that do not constitute knowledge is at least as important as the arguments themselves. I start that project in this chapter and return to it with greater force after presenting the arguments in the next chapter.

1.2   Two Kinds of (Allegedly) Justified but Unknown Belief

There are two classes of beliefs that do not constitute knowledge and which many philosophers contend are nevertheless justified: I will call these classes the unknown unknown and the known unknown for reasons that will become apparent. (It is a solecism to call a belief that does not constitute knowledge an 'unknown belief'. I hope that the convenience of the term outweighs its incorrectness.) Many, if not most, philosophers take there to be justified beliefs that are not members of these two classes, but just *which* beliefs are justified that do not constitute knowledge and are not members of the two classes is extremely controversial. The unknown unknown and known unknown beliefs are examples of allegedly justified beliefs whose status as such commands broad *intuitive* support. I will return to the matter of beliefs whose status as justified is not so intuitive in section 1.3.6.[1]

If the reader does not share the widespread intuition that either of the classes of beliefs are genuinely justified, or does not agree that the intuition *is* widespread, that is, of course, fine by me: I will be arguing that neither class of beliefs is genuinely justified, and I welcome partial agreement with that position at the outset. I will not attempt to define each of the classes *precisely;* I seek only to define their intuitive character in enough detail that, first, the reader will know which beliefs I am talking about, and, second, I can make a number of important points about the two classes, both in this section and for much of the rest of the book. I am not committed to even the possibility of such definitions. Of course, I am even less committed to a precise definition of a concept that encompasses knowledge, the unknown unknown and/or the known unknown beliefs, and possibly more beliefs as well. That is a job for my opponents, not for one who identifies justification and knowledge as I do.

1.2.1 The Unknown Unknown

Suppose that I have entered the land of fake dollar bills. A counterfeiting operation has established itself so successfully in a nearby neighborhood that almost all the currency in circulation is fake, although I suspect nothing. If I believe that the fake $10 bill that I was just handed in change is genuine, my belief is justified although false, orthodoxy maintains. Of course, I could be "lucky" (we will have more to say about such luck below) and end up with one of the few genuine bills in circulation. Because of my obliviousness to the counterfeiting operation and lack of awareness of how hard it is to come by a genuine bill in this neighborhood, I do not know that I have a $10 bill in hand, although I have a justified, true belief that I do, according to received wisdom—this is a Gettier case.[2] Similar examples of (allegedly—often understood hereafter) justified, false beliefs are easy to come by and occur often in actuality. Many, or even most, can be used to construct examples of justified, true beliefs that actually occur at least sometimes.

Someone who has this variety of justified belief does not know that he does not know; I will hence call such beliefs 'unknown unknown'. Upon minimal reflection, it is likely that I would believe that I knew that I had a genuine $10 bill whether that belief is true or false.[3] Whether I am a Gettier victim or not (whether my belief is true or false), if I came to know that I did not or had not known that I had a $10 bill—for example, by being informed of the prevalence of counterfeit bills in the area—I would also lose justification for my belief and, if rational, I would give up the belief itself.[4] Discussions of Gettier cases often stress the good luck that the Gettier victim enjoys—it is a lucky accident that his belief is true. This good luck is subsequent to *bad* luck, however, which is at least as noteworthy, although much less often noted.[5] It was bad luck that I was in the land of fake dollar bills, or the land of fake barns, or that my colleague had just sold his Ford despite my having such good evidence that he owned such a car.[6] The unknown unknown variety of justified belief, whether true or false, would have constituted knowledge but for unfortunate circumstances. (Of course, the false beliefs would not have been false in more fortunate circumstances.) The believer could have formed his belief in exactly the same *internal* way (his relevant mental states are the same) in different *external* circumstances—indeed, the kind of circumstances that are far more common in actuality—and his belief would have constituted knowledge.[7] I would know that I had a genuine $10 bill if I formed a belief that I did in the same way that I do in the land of fakes in normal circumstances. If I formed a belief that there was a barn over there just by looking in that direction from a distance in normal circumstances in which fake barns are absent, I would know that there was a barn over there. And if my colleague actually did own a Ford and had generated my evidence that he did in the regular way, I would know that he owned a Ford on the basis of that evidence alone if I were to so believe.

It is very plausible that the good luck in Gettier cases is what leads us to deny that the victim knows despite having a true and (allegedly) justified belief.[8] It is good luck that his belief is true. It is just as plausible, I suggest, that it is bad luck that leads us to call the unknown unknown category of justified beliefs, including the Gettier cases, *justified*. It is because the victim would have known but for his bad luck that we keep his epistemic virtue intact by employing this label. This suggests that any genuine concept of justification at work in our so labeling this category of justified belief is parasitic on the concept of knowledge. We only understand what it is to be justified in the appropriate sense because we understand what it is to know, and we extend the notion of justification to nonknowers only because they are would-be knowers. We grasp the circumstances—ordinary rather than extraordinary—in which the justified would know. Justification in the relevant sense is perhaps a disjunctive concept—it is knowledge or would-be knowledge. In light of these considerations alone, the suggestion that justification is a more fundamental notion than knowledge, that justification is what is *really* important in epistemology, is dubious.[9] These comments are, of course, mere suspicions—suspicions that I hope will gain strength throughout the book and to which we will return in section 1.3.5.[10]

We cannot characterize the unknown unknown beliefs simply as those that, although they do not constitute knowledge, are based on good reasons. This is an insufficiently discriminating characterization. Many philosophers will take a belief that one's ticket will not win a fair lottery to be based on good reasons, but such lottery beliefs are not unknown unknown beliefs. They would not amount to knowledge that one's ticket will not win even in normal circumstances, and so they cannot easily be used to construct Gettier cases. Lottery beliefs are members of the second category of allegedly justified but unknown beliefs discussed immediately below—the known unknown.[11]

If by 'based on good reasons' one means 'based on reasons sufficient to render a belief knowledge in normal circumstances', or if one denies that a belief that one's ticket will not win the lottery is based on good reasons since it would not constitute knowledge even in normal circumstances, then I do not have any quibble with the characterization of the unknown unknown beliefs as beliefs based on good reasons that do not constitute knowledge—because it does not clearly differ from my own more than terminologically. The claim that labeling the unknown unknown beliefs 'justified' employs a concept of justification that is parasitic on knowledge stands.[12]

1.2.2 The Known Unknown

It is sometimes thought that if a proposition p is known to be sufficiently probable, then one is justified in believing that p even if one does not know that *p*. The aforementioned example to which we will return in some detail below (section 2.1.2) in discussing the lottery paradox is the belief that one's ticket will not win the lottery. One does not know that one will not win the lottery, many will agree, but one is justified in believing that one will not win on the basis of knowing that it is extremely likely that one will not win. Someone who believes justifiably that he will not win and yet does not know that he will not also typically knows, or can know upon minimal reflection, that he does not know that he will not win. Hence, I call this second category of justified belief the known unknown beliefs. In section 2.1.2, I will examine and endorse an argument that beliefs that one will not win the lottery formed on probabilistic grounds are not justified; the argument's conclusion can and will be generalized to all such beliefs formed on merely probabilistic grounds.

An important class of beliefs that are examples of known unknown allegedly justified belief are beliefs formed by inference to the best explanation. Suppose that the total evidence one has supports one theory (which might be as small as a single proposition) over all rival theories, but that evidence is not sufficiently strong that one knows the theory to be true on the basis of that evidence; at best, one can know that the theory is very likely to be true. Many will say that that evidence might nevertheless be strong enough to justify belief in the winning theory whether it is true or false. (Although of course it *need* not be strong enough to justify belief; the evidence might be too weak in either quantity or the degree to which it outweighs evidence for rival theories to do that.)

One who believes a proposition *p* on the basis of an inference to the best explanation that falls short of providing him with knowledge that *p* will often know that he does not know, or at least could do so upon minimal reflection (he will often know upon reflection that he at best knows the theory to be highly probable). Just as one who forms a belief that *p* on explicitly probabilistic grounds in the relevant kind of case knows that *p* is probable, one who forms a belief that *p* through inference to the best explanation in the relevant kind of case knows *something*—namely that the evidence on balance supports *p* to a greater or lesser degree compared to such-and-such specified or unspecified rival theories, *and,* in many cases, that it is therefore likely to be true.

I will have more to say about the known unknown class of allegedly justified beliefs in particular in section 2.1.3, arguing (of course) that they are not justified after all. In section 2.3, however, I will argue that many beliefs that might *appear* to be known unknown, and hence unjustified, are in fact justified—that is, they constitute knowledge.

The concept of probability will be employed heavily throughout the book, and I should say something about its employment. Probability will function as something of a primitive for me—but not a *metaphysical* primitive. I will not talk about probability "out there in the world," but probability as it occurs in the mind—in the content of beliefs. This is not to say that I take probability to be something like "degree of belief"; I find such talk hard to understand. It is easy to understand someone's believing that there is a 50 percent chance of rain today, a belief that he might well express in the very probabilistic terms just used to characterize his belief. It is much harder, I suggest, to grasp what it is for a believer to believe the categorical proposition that it will rain today—but only half-believe it, as he half-believes the contradictory proposition that it will not rain today; again, it is rather easier to make sense of a believer who *fully* believes that there is a 50 percent chance that it will *not* rain today just as he fully believes the entailed opposing, but far from *contradictory*, probabilistic proposition. (Believers no doubt hold beliefs more or less confidently in the sense that they are more or less willing to abandon them in the face of opposition of one kind or another (evidential or social), but this is an entirely different matter from beliefs allegedly held to a greater or lesser degree.) I simply take there to be a difference between the *content* of the belief that p and the belief that probably p—distinct propositions are believed in each case, one of which contains a concept of probability, and one of which does not (assuming that p itself is not a probabilistic proposition). The relevant concept of probability that figures in such beliefs is certainly in some sense epistemic and also partially subjective. Given what we all know about fair lotteries, one can know that S has probably not won the lottery. On the other hand, someone whose "background knowledge" differs from one's own—someone who knows that the first nine digits of the winning ten-digit number match those on S's ticket, for example—can know that S probably *has* won the lottery (or, of course, that he actually has won, given yet more background knowledge), if we make appropriate assumptions about the particular lottery itself.

This degree of subjectivity means the notion of probability that figures in the content of the kind of belief that probably p that will concern us is implicitly relativized to the believer himself (or a larger or smaller group of believers of which he is a member; a couple of fellow researchers or the entire scientific community, for example)—he believes and knows that p is probable *for him*. Since knowledge entails truth, given that one subject knows that probably p and another knows that probably not p, we can infer that probably p and that probably not p.[13] On the reasonable assumption that probably not p entails not probably p, it *appears* that we can infer an explicit contradiction—that probably p and not probably p. The apparent contradiction is merely apparent if probability is relativized to individual believers. What is true is that p is probable for one subject and that not-p is probable for another subject (and, further, it is not the case that p is probable for the latter subject); that is all that we can infer from what both subjects know, although, in context, the relativization is often left implicit.

There are two respects in which I take the subjectivity of the relevant epistemic notion of probability to be only partial. First, if S has just two tickets in a million ticket lottery, but his friend falsely believes it to be a three ticket lottery (for whatever reason), *ceteris paribus* his friend does not know that S will probably win the lottery. Probabilistic knowledge must be itself grounded in knowledge, not mere belief. Second, even if one knows that S probably has not won, someone who knows that he probably *has* won (or categorically that he has won) based on his superior knowledge of the situation can legitimately contradict any claim that one makes that S has probably not won. There can be intersubjective disputes about the probability of a proposition even though both sides *know* contrary propositions to be true. Indeed, one side can, of course, win; should the side that knows that S probably has won on the basis of superior background knowledge provide that background knowledge to the other side, the other side will in many cases no longer know that S probably has not won (and so "lose") *even if he stubbornly persists in believing that S probably has not won*.

I will not characterize situations in which the probabilistic knowledge that is the subject of dispute is itself based on probabilistic knowledge, and in what superiority of background knowledge might consist if both sides know substantially *distinct* sets of propositions that are the basis for their knowledge of probabilistically contrary propositions. I hope to have said enough to characterize the epistemic notion of probability that I will employ in characterizing belief content throughout this work, and that is all that I aim to do since this work merely *uses* an epistemic notion of probability; it is not a central *subject* of the work.[14]

1.3 Five Concepts of Justification

Four of the five concepts of justification characterized below are coextensive with the concept of knowledge, I will argue in this chapter and the next, at least when those four concepts are assigned a clearly *epistemic* sense. There are no justified beliefs that do not amount to knowledge if one understands justified belief in these four ways, and all beliefs that constitute knowledge are justified in these four senses. Nevertheless, there are secondary ways of taking two of those concepts of justification (blameless belief and warrant) that we should take care not to confuse with justified belief; if we do confuse them, we will be concerned with an impure notion of justified belief, and consequently cannot hope to achieve a clear understanding of justified belief unmixed with other concepts entirely. I distinguish five rather than *seven* concepts of justification because the secondary, "generalized" concept of blameless belief is not of epistemological interest *except* insofar as we should take care not to confuse it with what *is* of epistemological interest and because it is not at all clear that *warrant* understood in its secondary sense has any but the *empty* extension, whether there are any warranted beliefs at all in the secondary sense of warrant.

Of those four concepts, the two that do *not* have further secondary senses that are epistemologically unimportant or are arguably empty—evaluative and deontological justification—are the central concepts of justification that I identify with knowledge and will be treated as such in later chapters. However, this should not be taken to mean that there are other, abandoned concepts of justification that I do *not* identify with knowledge. Blameless belief in its distinctively epistemic sense, and warrant (in its primary sense *if it is a coherent concept at all*) *are* concepts coextensive with the concept of knowledge.

The fifth concept of justification, which I call 'reasonableness', is not coextensive with the concept of knowledge; however, it is also not much like any concept of justified belief that epistemologists have employed since it is *parasitic* on the concept of knowledge, not a concept independent of the concept of knowledge, nor a concept that can be used to define knowledge—rather, it is itself defined in terms of knowledge. Reasonableness is discussed simply to make clear that it is justified belief as epistemologists have taken the notion that I insist simply *is* knowledge; there is at least one other *somewhat* similar epistemic notion not coextensive with knowledge, and perhaps it is even a notion of some philosophical importance, but it bears no more than a superficial similarity to justified belief as it has been discussed in contemporary epistemology.

1.3.1 Warrant

It is tempting to begin with an apparently neutral definition of justification as what Alvin Plantinga (1993a, b) calls *warrant*, leaving a more substantive characterization of justification to be developed after one has seen what fits Plantinga's definition. Justification as warrant (Plantinga rejects the *term* 'justification' because of its deontological connotations) is whatever it is that makes the difference between mere true belief and knowledge—what has to be added to true belief to achieve knowledge. Knowledge is belief that is (a) true and (b) has property X, which is warrant/justification by definition.

The apparent neutrality of this definition is merely apparent, however. It assumes, first, that knowledge can be defined (and defined in an illuminating way, in more epistemically primitive terms) and, second, that such a definition will include a component that does not entail truth, that specifies a property that false beliefs can share with true beliefs.[15] Both of these assumptions are questionable and have been questioned. Linda Zagzebski (1996) and Trenton Merricks (1995) have argued that whatever differentiates mere true belief from knowledge entails truth, and Merricks notes that many definitions of knowledge, such as Robert Nozick's (Nozick 1981), do not include a separable warrant component that does not entail truth.[16] Timothy Williamson (2000) has argued that knowledge is not definable at all and should be regarded as a conceptual primitive. As he notes, the definability of knowledge does not follow from the fact that knowledge entails truth; being red entails being colored, but no one expects to define being red as being colored plus something else. We make an analogous assumption if we assume that there is such a thing as warrant in Plantinga's sense.

I am sympathetic to Williamson's position; at the end of the next chapter, I will argue that Williamson's opposition to the project of defining knowledge in a more or less traditional manner is compatible with a commonsense *functionalism* about knowledge and will bolster his objections to that project with some of my own. *If* Williamson, Zagzebski, and others are wrong and knowledge can be defined in terms of a notion like Plantinga's warrant, then clearly the notion of justification that I wish to identify with knowledge cannot be warrant. Necessarily, warrant is entailed by, but does not entail, knowledge. Equally, if my arguments succeed, then warrant is not even extensionally equivalent to any of the notions of justification that I do identify with knowledge. Some of those seeking to identify a notion of warrant such that warranted true belief is knowledge have wanted to identify warrant with the evaluative conception of justification outlined below.[17] Since I will be arguing that evaluative justification is knowledge, at least some of my arguments need to be effective against at least these notions of warrant. One of my arguments will need to be modified to be so effective since it assumes that there are justified true beliefs that do not constitute knowledge; I will note the modification required. Some of my arguments simply do not apply to any notion of warrant that is *distinct* from knowledge.

The case against warrant that my arguments present is perhaps not as compelling as the case against other notions of justification, but, taken together, the arguments have enough persuasive force to rule out an evaluative notion of warrant. On the other hand, the notion of warrant is considerably less intuitive than a more orthodox notion of justification.[18] The unknown unknown beliefs, which provide intuitive support for the orthodox notions, do not provide intuitive support for the notion of warrant since those beliefs are *not* warranted. The unknown unknown true beliefs are *ex hypothesi* unwarranted since warrant solves the Gettier problem; *warranted* true beliefs constitute knowledge. Unknown unknown false beliefs are also, it seems, unwarranted since they have counterparts that are true. If the false beliefs were warranted, it is hard to see how their true counterparts would lack warrant, and hence it is hard to see why warrant would not give rise to Gettier problems after all.

The known unknown beliefs are no better at providing intuitive support for the notion of warrant. True beliefs formed on explicitly probabilistic grounds or on the basis of inference to the best explanation that fall short of knowledge are unwarranted by definition; once again, it is very hard to see how their false counterparts could be warranted. In short, neither of the two classes of allegedly justified beliefs that are supposed to provide illustrations of justification without knowledge provide even apparent illustrations of warrant without knowledge. The claim that there *is* a serviceable notion of warrant, even if it is supposed to do double duty as a component in the definition of knowledge *and* as a notion of evaluative justification, is (unsurprisingly) no more intuitive than the claim that knowledge is definable as truth plus something else. Warrant is a notion largely employed by externalists, and the main intuitive support that externalists of any stripe have is intuitive support for externalism about knowledge itself. Many intuitive cases of knowledge—cases of ordinary, unreflective, perceptual knowledge, for example—seem to require that knowledge is externalist in character. That such cases amount to knowledge seems to depend on features of the believer's external environment to which he need not have immediate and unproblematic access—whether he is in the land of fake barns or not, for example. But there is no intuitive support for warrant in such cases unless one finds it intuitive that there is such a thing before consideration of the cases.

So much for warrant as a property *distinct* from that of knowledge, a property that false beliefs can possess. This is what I referred to in the introduction to the section as the *secondary* sense of warrant, and it is what we will mean later in the book when we talk of warrant, for warrant in its *primary* sense simply *is* knowledge—as Plantinga (1997) himself states in responding to Merricks's (and Zagzebski's) arguments.[19] Plantinga's response is concessive, in substance if not in tone. He states that warrant comes in degrees, and the only false beliefs that have warrant have it to a suboptimal degree. What, then, is warrant to an optimal degree? Warrant that is "sufficient for knowledge"; since knowledge entails truth, optimal warrant entails truth. ('Optimal' is not Plantinga's own term, although he does say that false beliefs can only have '*some* warrant' [his emphasis]. *Full* warrant appears to entail knowledge, and hence truth.) That is about as clear an endorsement of the view that (full) warrant just is knowledge as one might imagine. Ultimately all we find in Plantinga's postulation of optimal warrant is *a definition of knowledge*. To suppose that there is such a thing as optimal warrant is to suppose that there is a definition of knowledge, and to supply a definition of optimal warrant is to supply a definition of knowledge.

What of Plantinga's partial warrant, of the suboptimal degrees of warrant that false beliefs can possess along with true beliefs that fall short of knowledge? It is beyond question that one can have a belief that meets some and *only some* of the conditions that would make it constitute knowledge. It is

questionable whether such beliefs are of much epistemological interest beyond the fact that they do not amount to what is of primary epistemological
interest—knowledge. Indeed, since there are *many* ways in which one's beliefs might fall short of having all that it takes to constitute knowledge, it is
perhaps mistaken to talk of a belief possessing only some *degree* of warrant
since such talk suggests a *linearity* that will be hard to find—it might well
be fruitless to attempt to arrange beliefs that fall short of knowledge into a
continuum of warrant leading from complete lack of warrant all the way to
knowledge itself. (Some might suggest that a notion of partial warrant will
be of some philosophical utility in the diagnosis and solution of epistemic
paradoxes such as the paradox of the preface and the lottery paradox; I will
address those paradoxes without need of such notions in the next chapter.)
When we consider warrant from this point on, it is full warrant that will be
our exclusive concern.

Warrant in its *secondary* sense—the only sense that will occupy us from
here on, largely to explore the properties that it would be required to have *if*
there were such a thing—is, then, arguably a concept that *no* beliefs satisfy.
Warrant in its *primary* sense includes all and only beliefs that constitute
knowledge *if and only if* knowledge is definable—a matter we will return to
in section 2.5.

1.3.2   The Deontological Conception

A deontological conception of justification supposes justification to be tied
to epistemic obligations—what one ought to believe, what one ought not
believe, what one is permitted to believe, what one is not permitted to
believe, what one is permitted not to believe, and so on. Philosophers who
have claimed that there are epistemic obligations have most commonly
taken those obligations to be negative—there are certain beliefs that one
should not have. For example, evidentialists claim that one should not
have beliefs that are not supported by one's evidence (Feldman and Conee
1985). Some philosophers have claimed that there are positive epistemic
obligations too: again, some evidentialists have claimed that one ought to
believe what one's evidence does support (ibid.).[20]

I use the term 'obligation' simply to denote deontic facts expressed by
statements such as that one should or should not believe such-and-such.
This is somewhat at odds with ordinary usage. Perhaps I should not have
believed that Santa Claus would visit on Christmas Eve when I was a child,

but it is exceptionally odd to say that I had an obligation not to believe that. In the ordinary sense of 'obligation', its connection to notions such as blameworthiness might be unbreakable. That connection is breakable if we use the term for the deontic facts alone, as I argue in section 1.3.4 below. That such deontic facts do not seem to entail the existence of obligations in the ordinary sense is, of course, not a phenomenon exclusive to belief. If I buy a very poor used car, then *ceteris paribus* I should not have bought the car. Equally, *ceteris paribus,* I had no obligation to refrain from making the purchase in any ordinary sense of 'obligation'.

I claim that beliefs justified in a deontological sense are those and only those that constitute knowledge. I claim that we human beings have a negative epistemic obligation: one ought not believe that *p* unless one knows that *p*, for any proposition *p*. Equivalently, one is permitted to believe that *p* only if one knows that *p*. I will not in general be concerned to argue that there are any positive epistemic obligations, and, indeed, I am inclined to think that the vast majority of beliefs that one ought to hold are such for nonepistemic reasons. Such positive doxastic obligations depend on what is important or interesting to oneself or others, among other considerations, and those notions of importance or interest are not epistemic notions. In section 2.1.3, I will in passing suggest one notable exception.

Many philosophers have assumed that to adopt a deontological notion of justification is also to adopt an *internalist* notion of justification (Sosa 1999, for example)—that one's belief is or is not justified is something that one can tell solely by introspection. Indeed, many have assumed that a deontological understanding of justification provides a motivation or *the* motivation for internalism (Goldman 1999; Plantinga 1993b).[21] In the next section, I will discuss to what extent my view of justification as knowledge is internalist, externalist, or uncommitted to either position. I will also discuss and endorse Hilary Kornblith's view that externalism and deontology are quite compatible and will apply his conclusions to my own view of justification.

Some philosophers, such as William Alston (1985), do not believe in deontological justification since they think that it entails a degree of voluntary control over what beliefs we form that we do not possess. Such arguments have been ably criticized by others in my view (Steup 2001a; Kornblith 2001; Feldman 2001), and I will not consider them here, merely noting that I agree with these critics that we do not need any problematic level of voluntary control of our beliefs for there to be epistemic obligations. Indeed, I will not argue that there are any epistemic obligations (such a task seems as fruitless as arguing that there are moral obligations), but will argue simply that if there are any, then they have the direct relation to knowledge that I propose.

Alvin Goldman (1999) associates a deontological conception of justification with the notion of *guidance;* epistemic duties, if there are any, are supposed to play a role in how one forms one's beliefs. An identification of justification with knowledge enables the believer to be so guided. Although we perhaps do not always know that we know what we know, and perhaps sometimes *cannot* know that we know, we nevertheless are *often* able to know that we know—or that we do not know. If we find ourselves believing theories that we know we do not know to be true, although we take ourselves to know them to be best supported by the available evidence, we can retreat to the more modest belief. If we find ourselves believing that our house has not burned down while we were on vacation, we can correct ourselves and believe that it is merely very *probably* intact. If we find ourselves believing everything we read in the newspaper, although we know that identifiable portions of it are unlikely to express knowledge on the part of the reporter (and so beliefs thereby produced will fail to constitute knowledge), we can retreat to what we *do* know, which might be as much as that there is a good chance that what was reported is the case, or as little as that it was reported to be the case.

If we embrace externalism about justified belief, whether we take justified belief to be identical to knowledge *or not,* we will have to accept that our attempts to believe only what is justified are *fallible.* It is always possible that we will fail to believe justifiably because of *external* bad luck. The world can fail to cooperate with our attempt to grasp it, in a fashion to which we do not have ready doxastic access (either globally—any standard skeptical scenario involving evil demons or dreaming will serve[22]—or locally—fake barns and such), although we would have grasped it unproblematically had the world been more cooperative. Our internal *but inaccessible* cognitive procedures might also be unreliable in a manner that is not transparent to us and might prevent our beliefs from being justified—our memory or senses can let us down. *Any* externalist can and should reject the demand that there be some fully general rule of belief formation that can necessarily be followed without error. That there is no such rule is in effect what I am arguing for in this chapter and the next. Moreover, there is no need for such a rule; a rule we can follow (*do* follow, much of the time)—believe only what is justified, *that is* believe only what one knows, on my view—is in working order, even though it is fallible since the circumstances in which we are prone to err in following the rule are *exceptional,* or at least will be exceptional provided we take care (*and* provided that we are not the inhabitant of a demon world, of course—an assumption that any externalist about justification makes).

1.3.3 The Evaluative Conception

I identify evaluative justification with knowledge just as I did deontological justification. Many have followed Alston in distinguishing the evaluative conception of justification from the deontological conception, of which he is suspicious as we noted above. A belief is justified in the evaluative sense if it is "a good thing from the epistemic point of view" (Alston 1985, 329). Since few would want to say that forming a justified belief—in any proposition on any topic—is a good thing *per se* from *any* point of view, perhaps it would be better to characterize an evaluatively justified belief as one that is not a *bad* thing from an epistemic point of view.[23] Characterizing *unjustified* belief implicitly by defining justified belief is arguably what is central.

Endorsing an evaluative conception of justification does not commit one to claiming that one ought to pursue only beliefs that are a good thing from the epistemic point of view. Only if one endorses a conception of justification that is both evaluative and deontological is one so committed. At its most general, what is a good thing from an epistemic point of view, for Alston at least, involves aiming at maximizing true belief and minimizing false belief. He claims that this is "uncontroversial" (Alston 1993, 535), and many philosophers have assumed without argument that truth maximization and falsity minimization are a primary or the primary epistemic goal (or goals). More must be said, Alston tells us, to identify a general epistemic goal that is *epistemic*. Truth, after all, is perhaps a supremely good thing from an epistemic point of view, but justification cannot be identified with truth since it is not *internal* enough, he says (Alston 1993, 1985, again).

I claim that what is justified in the evaluative sense is knowledge—it is knowledge that is the supremely good thing from an epistemic point of view and, unlike truth perhaps, it is epistemic enough to *be* justification.

Indeed, truth cannot be identified with justification for an entirely different reason from that which Alston cites—it has nothing to do with its lack of internal accessibility. The simple reason is that a true belief need not constitute knowledge (it might simply be a lucky guess), hence truth is not good enough for justification. Furthermore, it is not or should not be uncontroversial that our primary epistemic goal is a combination of truth maximization and falsity minimization.

The reason for this is that, as I will argue, the allegedly justified beliefs in the known unknown category of beliefs are not, in fact, justified. If a justified belief is one formed in serving the aim of maximizing true belief and minimizing false belief, the known unknown beliefs are apparently justified. If one knows (or could know upon minimal reflection) that it is highly probable that p—for example, that it is highly probable that one's ticket will lose the lottery—then in forming the belief that one will lose, one serves the aim of maximizing truth while minimizing falsity, it appears since it is by hypothesis highly probable that the belief one has formed is true. Similarly, if one knows that the best available evidence supports a theory T over its rivals to such a degree that T is (merely) *highly likely* to be true, then in forming a belief that T *is* true, although one's evidence is not so good that one knows that to be the case, one is highly likely to have formed a true belief and so, it appears, to have served the aim of maximizing truth and minimizing falsity. This is not to say that there is *no* interpretation of truth maximization/falsity minimization consistent with saying both that this goal somehow determines, or is closely connected to, evaluative justification and that the known unknown beliefs are not really justified. It is to say that it should not be uncontroversial that there is such an interpretation—it should not be assumed that there is one. I will offer an alternative account of what is a good thing from the epistemic point of view in what follows.

Another assumption is almost as common as the assumption that truth maximization/falsity minimization is a primary epistemic goal—the assumption that a central fact about belief is that it *aims* at truth (see, e.g., Williams 1973, 148, cited in Ginet 2001). Known unknown beliefs again suggest that this is not so.[24] If belief aims at truth, then the belief that one will lose the lottery or that a theory such as T is true will, in almost all cases, succeed in fulfilling that central aim, and so should be impeccably formed, that is, justified. If, as I will argue, the known unknown beliefs are *not* justified, and are not justified because they do not constitute knowledge, we should rather say that belief aims at knowledge.[25]

There are many truths that it is not in one's interests to believe *or know* because they are unimportant, uninteresting, tasteless, upsetting, or dangerous. One needs to square this fact with the claim that truth maximization is a primary epistemic goal if one wishes to support that claim. One is likely to do so by claiming that it *is* in one's *epistemic* interests to believe such truths, but not in one's nonepistemic interests, which can easily outweigh one's epistemic interests. But there is no need to cast epistemic goals in terms of *maximizing* anything once we have abandoned naked truth as the center of our epistemic life. We can simply talk of the aim or goal of individual beliefs and of belief in general. Alston (1993) says that we cannot define justification as what serves our most general epistemic goals since that is truth, which is clearly not what justification amounts to (since it is not "epistemic enough"). But we can so define justification if belief aims at knowledge rather than truth. There is no temptation to bring truth into our account of justification in a suitably *epistemic* way by refining the notion of truth maximization since it is entailed by knowledge, a paradigm of the epistemic.

Talk of the *aim* of belief is more than a little obscure, as is talk of distinctively *epistemic* goals itself. I would like to clarify such talk by saying that the *function* of belief is to be knowledge; that is what belief is *for*, in terms of whatever notion of design or purpose one wants to apply to human beings, their states, and faculties. Belief can serve many functions, but *the* function—the proper function, if you like—is to be knowledge. And the proper function of the faculties that produce beliefs is to produce beliefs that constitute knowledge. If this is right, defining justification or warrant in terms of the proper function of those faculties or of the beliefs themselves is just to define justification as knowledge rather than as a more primitive *component* of knowledge (namely, warrant), contra Plantinga (1993a).

How do I propose to argue that justified belief in the evaluative *and* deontological senses is knowledge? A number of my arguments establish a conclusion statable using either conception of justification (the assertion and lottery arguments in particular). All of my arguments indirectly support a dual conclusion, however, since the identification of one of the two forms of justification with knowledge gives rise to a subsidiary argument that the other form must also be identified with knowledge. The reader should not assign too much weight to the conclusions of those subsidiary arguments; what one gets out of an argument is, after all, in a sense just what one puts in. Once one divorces the notion of epistemic obligation from the notion of blame, as in an important sense I will below, it is not too much of a stretch to connect tightly a belief that would be a bad thing from an epistemic point of view with a belief that one should not form in *some* important sense of 'should'.

First, let us see that if deontological justification is knowledge, then so is evaluative justification. I shall assume that justification in any important evaluative sense does not require *more* than knowledge—too few of our beliefs would be justified on a more stringent conception for the notion of evaluative justification to play the important epistemic role that it is supposed to play.[26] Suppose that it requires less than knowledge. Suppose that my belief that p is justified in the evaluative sense, that it satisfies a primary or the primary epistemic goal, but that I do not know that p. Suppose further that deontological justification is knowledge, and so my belief is not justified in the deontological sense. Then, I ought not believe that p although I am satisfying primary epistemic goals in so doing. That seems completely mysterious.[27] If there are epistemic obligations at all, it is conceivable (although false, I suggest below) that fulfilling primary epistemic goals requires going beyond one's epistemic obligations, but it is inconceivable that one might simultaneously fulfill those goals and violate those obligations. If there are epistemic obligations at all, one is surely epistemically *permitted* to fulfill primary epistemic goals. Indeed, it is quite plausible that one is obligated to *pursue* those goals in some sense, even if one is not obligated to fulfill them. So, I contend, if epistemic obligations are as stringent as I claim that they are, the deontological and evaluative conceptions of justification coincide.

Now I will argue that if evaluative justification is knowledge, then deontological justification is too. This argument relies on the assumption that there *are* epistemic obligations, and something must first be said about what such obligations require.

Typically, as noted above, deontological conceptions have been associated with internalist theories of justification. Is my view externalist or internalist? Strictly speaking, it is neutral. Since justification is identified with knowledge, it is as externalist or internalist as knowledge itself, on which I do not *need* to take a position for a lot of what I say in this book to succeed. However, very few philosophers nowadays hold an internalist view of knowledge. Almost all would agree that there are possible (and likely actual) pairs of thinkers (interworld or intraworld) who form a belief with a given content p and who are in exactly similar relevant mental states— and have *access* to all the same relevant mental states—one of whom knows that p, the other of whom does not. In section 1.2.1, I suggested that all the unknown unknown, allegedly justified beliefs can provide examples. Some- one with such a belief would have known if entirely external circumstances had been different.[28] Consequently, one does not have *infallible* access to whether or not one knows.[29] But only a militant Cartesian would claim otherwise, and there are few of those left.

On the other hand, my view avoids some of the classic problems for the most prominent externalist theory of justification, reliabilism. My view does not even appear to entail that a clairvoyant who doubts that he is capable of reliably forming the beliefs that he does in fact reliably form forms justified beliefs since it is very plausible that such a clairvoyant's beliefs do not constitute knowledge (Bonjour 1985). Indeed, it is obviously consistent with my view that no clairvoyant or chicken-sexer, however confident in his beliefs, forms justified beliefs since it is consistent with my view that these characters' beliefs do not constitute knowledge.

Although it is common to associate deontological conceptions of justi- fication with internalism about justification, and many externalists about justification (of which I am an exotic example, given the above) disavow any epistemic obligations, Hilary Kornblith (2001) is a notable exception. I mention his views not to endorse them wholeheartedly (although I have no particular objections to his views), but to illustrate how deontologi- cal obligations, at least if divorced from the notion of blame, are perfectly compatible with externalism about justification, and further with the iden- tification of deontological justification and knowledge. There might well be other, equally good, ways to explicate the deontic facts that are compatible with externalism. I commit myself simply to the claim that deontic facts ex- ist and that there is no reason to think this incompatible with externalism, as Kornblith illustrates.

Kornblith argues that we should understand justification as an *ideal* state, one determined by the nature of the human mind and its capacities, but not any *individual's* mind or its capacities. Some—perhaps all—humans will be more or less incapable of living up to that ideal in some of the situations in which they form (or fail to form) or renounce (or fail to renounce) beliefs.[30] He says:

An appropriate human ideal must in some ways be responsive to human capacities. Ideals are meant to play some role in guiding action, and an ideal that took no account of human limitations would thereby lose its capacity to play a constructive action-guiding role. At the same time, our ideals cannot be so closely tied to what particular individuals are capable of that we fail to recognize that some individuals at some times are incapable of performing in ideal ways. There is a large middle ground here, and it is here that reasonable ideals are to be found. (Kornblith 2001, 238)

For Kornblith, evaluative justification is a matter of satisfying primary epistemic goals—or, as we might just as well say, ideals. Provided that we understand those ideals as *humanly* possible, at least in principle, and we adopt Kornblith's idealized understanding of deontological justification, we have a way to argue from claims about evaluative justification to counterpart claims concerning deontological justification. On my view, we ought to live up to the ideal—knowledge—that is the aim of belief, however difficult (or even "impossible" *in practice*) that might be in particular circumstances, and however much constant struggle and vigilance is accompanied by inevitable lapses.

Even if a deontological conception of justification has been, rightly or wrongly, largely regarded as the province of *internalist* theories, internalists have not wanted to concede evaluative justification to externalists, regarding justification in all important senses as internalist in nature. For an internalist, a belief is justified in virtue of conforming to internally accessible epistemic standards of some kind. Those standards might be entirely individualistic or subjective. Justification is a matter of conforming to what, at least upon reflection of the appropriate kind, the believer himself takes to be the proper methods of belief formation (Foley 1993). Conforming to those standards is perhaps just a matter of thinking that one is conforming to those standards—at least upon reflection of the appropriate kind. On the other hand, the internalist's standards for properly formed belief might be at least partially universal. Forming justified beliefs might be a matter, for all believers, of forming only beliefs that "cohere" in some specified sense with one's prior beliefs. Or it might be a matter of assigning only such confidence to propositions as the probability calculus dictates (via Bayes' theorem, for instance) in the light of one's prior assignments of probability/degree of confidence. One need not have *infallible* access to the fact that one has or has not conformed to such standards. However, for an internalist, access to the standards and one's having conformed or not to them is much easier than access to externalist standards. A Gettier victim, for example, has a justified belief for an internalist, and there is no obstacle to his awareness of that fact; that one's belief is warranted is much harder to ascertain, as is the fact that one's belief was formed by a reliable process, and it is certainly harder to ascertain that one's belief constitutes knowledge (although that is not by any means impossible for an externalist of any stripe).

Insofar as an internalist notion of justification is a competitor to my own, my arguments that justification is knowledge in both deontological and evaluative senses will work without modification against internalism. Moreover, since on my view there is only a *negative* obligation to refrain from belief unless one knows (with one exception noted in section 2.1.3), most varieties of internalism have unacceptable consequences. If one has unjustified beliefs, inferring further beliefs from them will by and large result in yet more unjustified beliefs no matter what standards—one's own upon reflection, the coherentist's, the subjective Bayesian's—one employs.[31] What one should do is abandon the prior unjustified beliefs, whether it is apparent to one or not (even upon reflection) that one should do so; they are a bad thing from an epistemic point of view. Most externalists are likely to endorse this claim—it does not depend upon identifying justification and knowledge.[32]

Some might suggest that internalist justification is *not* intended to be a competitor to externalist theories of evaluative (and deontological) justification, including my own.[33] Rather, externalist and internalist standards of justification can coexist. There are beliefs that one ought or ought not form by internalist standards and beliefs that are a bad thing or not a bad thing from an internalist point of view. There are also beliefs that are a bad thing or not a bad thing from an externalist point of view (and—if one is inclined to deontological externalism—that one ought or ought not form from such a point of view). Externalist and internalist standards will not in general declare all the same beliefs justified, but this is not in itself a problem on the dualist view: some beliefs are justified by both standards, some by one or the other, and some by neither—and what is so bad about that?

An internalist might even concede that I will be able to argue effectively that justification is knowledge in the *externalist* senses of evaluative and deontological justification—but so much the worse for externalism and so

much the better for internalism. Internalist justification is the only justification there is; externalists simply confuse justification and knowledge.

I need to dispatch this devious internalist before I even mount my arguments lest it seem impossible to argue that justification is knowledge in
every important sense, as I intend to do. The position is, I suggest, untenable if one set of standards always "wins" in the event of conflict—and I
suggest that externalist standards, whatever one takes them to be, always
win. Suppose that one's preferred internalist standards led to beliefs that
were unacceptable by whatever externalist standards the justification dualist is willing to countenance: beliefs that are false, or beliefs that are the
result of processes that at least generally yield false beliefs (processes that are
unreliable), or beliefs that do not constitute knowledge. One would abandon those beliefs *if one could.* If one *discovered* such a conflict, one's discovery
would arguably lead one to abandon the conflicting beliefs in the light of
internally accessible standards. A discovered putative conflict between internalist and externalist standards would be no such thing since the externalist
standards have internalist reflections. Of course, the internalist will say, one
should not retain a belief that one *believes* to be false, or that one believes to
be the result of an unreliable process, or that one believes not to constitute
knowledge (what he says will depend upon the externalist standards he is
willing to acknowledge); but these are internalist standards after all.

However, if one does not discover such a conflict, but merely contem-
plates its possibility, it is *still* intuitive to say that were that possibility
realized, it would be a bad thing; one should not retain the conflicting belief
even if it conforms to internalist standards. And if one actually thinks that
some of one's beliefs do violate the externalist standards that one is willing to countenance, but one does not know just which beliefs do so, the
verdict is the same: one has beliefs that are a bad thing from an epistemic
point of view, and one should abandon them, if only one could. Such judgments about undiscovered conflicts are much harder for the justification
dualist to explain. The dualist's internally accessible rules of belief formation are entirely subordinate to the external standards: beliefs formed in
accord with such rules are not a bad thing from the epistemic point of view
and one ought to follow them *only* if the beliefs thus formed live up to
the external standards of truth, reliability, or knowledge. It is the external
standards, then, that determine the only notions of justification there are.
("Rationality" is sometimes spoken of as though it is an internalist alterna-

tive to externalist justification. In light of the above and what is to follow in section 2.4, I contend that such rationality is a chimera. A rational belief is no more or less than a justified belief—that is, a belief that constitutes knowledge.)

It is likely that internalists, whether justification dualists or not, will be unmoved by this argument. I will return to the status of internalism about justification in section 2.4. Many find internalism intuitive; I will in that section partially acknowledge and partially explain away internalism's intuitive appeal. The intuitions that have led to many internalist theories are, I will suggest, entirely correct—in a sense. In a sense, intuitive internalism is not just consistent with my view that justification is knowledge, it is a *consequence* of it—in all its supporting detail, at least. Explaining why that is so will also involve explaining why internalists have misinterpreted internalist intuitions. *Soi-disant* internalism is not intuitive, and it is without intuitive support once one sees that an intuitive internalism is in fact a consequence of my heavily externalist view of justification. The arguments against orthodox internalism in section 2.4 are much more persuasive than the argument above, which is likely only to appeal to committed externalists (indeed, it will not be news to them, I imagine).

1.3.4 Justification as Blamelessness

The remaining conceptions of justification that I discuss below I consider in part to distinguish them from those discussed above and to argue that they are much less central notions of justification, if indeed they deserve the name 'justification' at all. What one cannot have, I suggest, is a satisfactory notion of justification that satisfies all or most of the conceptions that I discuss—particularly if one tries to develop a notion of justification that combines a *generalized,* not distinctively epistemic conception of blameless belief with any of the others, a point that many externalists (Plantinga, for example) have in effect stressed. Toward the end of this section, I will suggest that a distinctively epistemic conception of blameless belief—what I earlier referred to as blameless belief in the *primary* sense—is coextensive with the concept of knowledge.

Externalist theories of justification entail that many actual and possible believers have beliefs for which they cannot be blamed which are nevertheless unjustified. Goldman (1988) gives the example of believers who grow up in a "scientifically benighted" society who form some of their beliefs—

beliefs, moreover, that are crucial to whether they achieve or fail to achieve goals important to them—by worthless manipulation of zodiacal signs. Similar examples are easy to construct. There is almost no end to the crazy conclusions at which one might routinely arrive whose craziness it is practically impossible for one to recognize because it is inconceivable for people in one's social circumstances to believe anything different. Another problem that externalists worry about is what Sosa (1991b) calls 'the new evil-demon problem'. On many versions of reliabilism, a thinker globally deceived by an evil demon or who is a brain in a vat will have very few beliefs that are justified since they are not arrived at by the relevant kind of reliable process.

Goldman is happy to define a notion of a *weakly* justified belief that is more or less coextensive with blameless yet ill-formed belief (strong and weak justification are contraries) and that the zodiacal believers (and brains in vats) live up to, reserving 'strong justification' for justification in the epistemically important sense that concerns him. There are indefinitely many properties that some beliefs have and others lack that render the beliefs that have them good in some way connected more or less strongly with arriving at the truth. Goldman's strong and weak justification are two points on this continuum (even the zodiacal believers do not believe that they are forming beliefs via a process with an excellent chance of arriving at false belief, a "virtue" captured by Goldman's definition of weak justification). Hartry Field (1998) has noted that attempts to pick a point on this continuum and regard it as genuine justification give the impression that one is searching for some "justificatory fluid" that is sprayed on some beliefs and not others. He embraces the view that none of these competing notions are objectively any better than the others, a view he calls 'epistemological non-factualism'.[34] (It is the position of this book that an emphasis on truth-maximization is largely responsible for Field's skepticism. There is a unique justificatory fluid on my view, after all—knowledge.)

I am inclined, then, to regard Goldman's position as overly concessive. Its concessiveness is largely terminological, but it is the kind of terminological choice that leads one to carve out a multitude of notions of "justification" in logical space, and leads ultimately to Fieldian skepticism. Better to say that blamelessness is one thing and justification another, and that to call a belief unjustified is not to call it blameworthy. The new evil-demon problem is generated by a failure to recognize the distinction. For sure, if there are epistemic obligations at all, one *ought* to form only epistemically blameless beliefs, but this obligation should arise as a consequence of a more stringent obligation (as it certainly does on my view). Blamelessness can hardly be taken to be a primary epistemic goal—any purported epistemic goal that the zodiacal believers live up to qua zodiacal believers is much too modest to be central to our epistemic lives.

On anyone's view, beliefs can be blame*worthy* in many ways that are not distinctively epistemic; one certainly might blame a potential criminal for *knowing* all kinds of things about one's finances, after all, which is to blame him for having some of the beliefs that he has. What, then, is the distinctively epistemic sense of blame and blamelessness? What beliefs does *Reason alone* demand that we hold—or, rather, demand that we *not* hold? I take this chapter and the next to be about providing an answer to that question, and about arguing for the claim that Reason alone demands that we believe only that which we know, that is, that we not believe what we do not know. Stating the view defended here in this fashion rather removes some of its apparent heterodoxy, I suggest. How many philosophers hold— or *have held*—such a view? A large number, indeed; it would seem to be the orthodox view, not even worthy of discussion, throughout most of the history of epistemology except for the last few decades (Plato, Descartes, Berkeley, Locke . . .). Henceforth, I shall talk of blamelessness so called in its secondary sense, that which it is important to distinguish from justified belief; however, the primary sense that *is* knowledge should be borne in mind.

(It is not quite true that philosophers of the past had nothing good to say about beliefs that do not amount to knowledge. Descartes [1996] granted that his beliefs prior to his temporarily falling prey to radical skeptical doubts were "probable opinions." Of course, he was after "firm and lasting knowledge," and probable opinions were not good enough for him. Bertrand Russell [1912], on the other hand, held that the vast majority of our beliefs are and must be mere probable opinions [the exceptions being mathematical and logical beliefs], but probable opinions are perfectly acceptable beliefs. In other words, both Descartes and Russell relegated almost all beliefs, temporarily in the former case and permanently in the latter, to known unknown status—we could know them to be merely probable and know them not to be knowledge. Russell regarded them as justified, and Descartes regarded them as unjustified; only Descartes thought that he could transform his former probable opinions into knowledge. A serious question for each philosopher is whether either were entitled to classify their beliefs even as probable opinions by their own lights since what is probable for one is, we suggested earlier in this chapter and will suggest again in chapter 4, determined not by what one rationally or irrationally believes but by what one *knows*. If one has very little knowledge, then very little will be probable for one.)

An externalist account of justification that endorses the existence of epistemic obligations faces the new evil demon/benighted society "problems" to an even greater degree than nondeontological externalists. It is conceivable that there is *no* connection between evaluative justification and blame, but there is surely *some* connection between deontological justification and blame. If you do not do what you ought to do, then, in at least some situations, you can be held to account on that basis.

Surely no externalist about justification faces this kind of problem as acutely as I do. I am not casting apparent aspersions solely on brains in vats or readers of runes, but on every believer, at least some of the time. Here is perhaps the worst case. We can have justified beliefs about the future, which on my view amounts to the fact that we can know many things about the future. You believe that you will meet me at the airport tomorrow and act on this belief in typical ways—you tell me that you will meet me there, and so on. But you drop dead this evening. I will not hold you to your obligation to *act,* to pick me up at the airport. But you did violate your epistemic obligations, on my view. You did not know that you would pick me up at the airport (although you would have known in more fortunate circumstances), and so, according to my view, you should not have believed that you would so act. How callous!

Such examples need not involve the future, of course. You believe that I live in a city. But *I* dropped dead five minutes ago, so I do not live anywhere, and your belief is false and so does not constitute knowledge. You ought not believe that I live in a city, although you once knew that I did (just ten minutes ago), and you could not be *expected* to be aware of the change in circumstances. Indeed, if I dropped dead a sufficiently small time ago, it will be *physically impossible* for you to realize that you must change your beliefs so as to live up to your epistemic obligations. That I regard standard examples of Gettier victims (and their unlucky counterparts with false beliefs) as in violation of their epistemic obligations seems almost trivial by comparison.

(It is rather strange for *any* externalist to regard the unknown unknown beliefs as justified [we have already seen that proponents of warrant cannot so regard them, largely by design]. What determines evaluative justification for an externalist is adherence to a set of epistemic standards that are external to the believer's mind. An unknown unknown belief is justified in part because of *ignorance*. The naive possessor of a genuine or fake dollar bill in the land of fake dollar bills is allegedly justified in believing his bill genuine only because he is ignorant of the local counterfeiting operation. If he became aware of that operation, he would no longer be justified in believing that his bill was genuine. It is a puzzling *external* epistemic goal that one achieves through ignorance but which one fails to meet by subsequently acquiring knowledge. And this is not a special case—*all* of the unknown unknown, allegedly justified beliefs have this characteristic.[35] An internalist—for example, a coherentist—has no problem here since the internalist's epistemic standards are entirely determined by his internal states, which obviously change when ignorance is removed, and in ways that clearly can, and often do, deprive, for instance, a formerly coherent set of beliefs of their coherence.)

With the blamelessness–justification distinction in hand, a deontological externalist has a ready response to the new evil-demon problem. A deontological externalist should be as much of a fallibilist about epistemic obligations as he is about justification itself. Brains in vats and zodiacal believers are not in a position to know that their beliefs are unjustified— nor are they in a position to know what they should (or, more relevantly, should not) believe. Brains in vats and zodiacal believers cannot—at least some of the time—live up to epistemic ideals or recognize what those ideals demand (although they might *think* that they can), and we cannot blame them for that (even if pure reason can). This does not remove their obligations. Often we have to teach people, particularly children, what their obligations (epistemic and otherwise) are, and often they are not capable of recognizing, or living up to, those obligations until we do. But we do not *create* those obligations by our instruction; we help them by making them aware of obligations they have that are already in effect. The obligation– blameworthiness distinction is needed to make sense of instructing people in what they ought to do—or believe.[36]

My kind of deontological externalism simply extends this story about brains in vats and zodiacal believers to all of us, at least some of the time. Just as a conflation of the distinction between blamelessness and justification can explain why some feel that a brain in a vat has many justified beliefs, that same conflation can explain the judgment that the ignorant in the land of fake dollar bills justifiably believe that they have genuine dollar bills.[37] We are all such that we sometimes are mistaken about our epistemic obligations and in such a way that it is in practice impossible for us to recognize that this is so. In practice, but not in principle—as Kornblith says, our epistemic obligations are ideals, but they are constrained by human capacities. Someone in the land of fake dollar bills is in principle capable of recognizing that he does not know that his bill is genuine (he just needs to check out the criminality of his neighborhood a little more thoroughly), just as the brain in a vat is in principle capable of living up to his epistemic obligations (he just needs to get out of his vat and get a life). You could have lived up to your obligations with regard to your belief that you would pick me up at the airport by *not dying,* just as a zodiacal believer could, in ideal conditions, come to realize that his astrological upbringing was worthless. The constraints placed upon our epistemic obligations by human capacities are very loose in the cases that are problematic for any deontological externalist—but the airport and fake bill cases are not *more* of a problem for me than the brain in a vat case is for any deontological externalist. Some possible and actual situations prevent us from realizing what our obligations are, but most of us are not in those situations most of the time, and it is humanly possible to get out of these situations or not get into them in the first place. I do not, after all, require that everyone should believe all the logical consequences of their beliefs as certain versions of evidentialism notoriously do, as Kornblith stresses (Feldman and Conee 1985).

A fallibilist about knowledge should say that even if we cannot infallibly know whether or not we know, we *often* can tell whether we know. A fallibilist about epistemic obligations should say the same. On my view, this is easy. Since we can often know that we know or know that we do not know, we can often know what we ought not believe—that which we do not know. The connection between epistemic obligation and what humans are capable of *in practice* is a loose fit, but the two go together for most of us most of the time. This brings us to the connection between *praiseworthiness* and epistemic obligation. Once again, the connection is loose: we do not praise people for failing to form any of a number of unjustified beliefs that they could form. One can, however, say this: if someone violates his obligations, he is not generally praiseworthy. Forming known unknown, allegedly justified beliefs is a violation of epistemic obligations on my view.

Consequently, believing that one has not won the lottery or that one will not die in a wreck on the highway or some scientific (or philosophical) theory that is best supported by one's evidence but not to such an extent that one knows it to be true is not generally praiseworthy.

Undoubtedly, such unjustified beliefs are commonplace as are their unknown unknown counterparts. This is not an objection to my view. Everyone thinks that unjustified beliefs are common, and everyone thinks that many people violate their obligations (of whatever kind) on a regular basis. As in any branch of philosophy that attempts to delineate our obligations (ethics being a central example), we are only loosely constrained by what others (philosophers and nonphilosophers) *take* to be their obligations, and we are only loosely constrained by the observed frequency with which people live up to what we conclude their obligations are. It is quite conceivable that regular violations are the norm in some epistemic situations, just as in some moral situations. Moreover, in epistemic situations as in moral situations, we should expect that the violations of some will encourage the violations of others, leading to localized epistemic scandals to which the protagonists are oblivious.

1.3.5 Justification as Reasonableness, or The Bit Where You Take It Back, Part I

It has been noted that 'justified' is rarely, if ever, applied to beliefs in everyday speech, the term being more commonly applied to actions, and that 'reasonable' is a term that is used of beliefs in much the way that philosophers use the term 'justified'. Surely, one might object at this point, people are talking about *something* when they talk of reasonable yet false (and therefore unknown) beliefs.[38]

I agree. This is no reason to think that reasonableness can be identified with justification in the philosophers' sense, however. For justification is supposed primarily to be a property of beliefs, and reasonableness can be understood as a property of beliefs only in a derivative sense; a sense that is defined *in terms* of knowledge rather than a sense that expresses an appropriate conceptual constituent of a definition of knowledge or a sense that expresses a concept substantially independent of knowledge, as epistemologists generally understand justification. Reasonableness in *one* sense is, I suggest, primarily a property of *persons*—a belief is reasonable in the circumstances in which it is held if a reasonable person would or could hold it in those circumstances (shades of "responsibilist" virtue epistemology [Zagzebski 1996]). The notion of a reasonable *person* is understood in terms of knowledge; he is one whose belief-forming faculties and habits (e.g., inferential habits) are such as to deliver knowledge when conditions are right. Of course, reasonable people are sometimes, through no fault of their own, in the wrong conditions, and then they form unjustified beliefs—unjustified on my view since they do not constitute knowledge. (The notion of a reasonable person and the derivative notion of belief are clearly notions that do come in *degrees*, depending on, for instance, just how easily one finds oneself in the wrong conditions, sometimes in ways for which one is very much responsible.) Those beliefs are nevertheless reasonable by definition. One who aims at knowledge and who is successful for the most part thereby achieves reasonableness—reasonableness is not an independent epistemic goal (it is not evaluative justification) and neither is there an obligation to be reasonable distinct from the obligation to believe only if one knows (it is not deontological justification). Not everyone who believes blamelessly is reasonable; remember the zodiacal believer—reasonableness is not blamelessness. (Neither, obviously, can it be used to define knowledge—it is not warrant.)

This characterization of reasonableness is very much of a piece with my suggestion in section 1.2.1 that our understanding of the notion of justification allegedly present in the unknown unknown beliefs is parasitic on our understanding of knowledge—it is would-be knowledge, so to speak. Known unknown beliefs are simply not reasonable even in this sense since they would not constitute knowledge even if conditions were right. (Although those who form beliefs in theories that they do not know to be true might be blameless since they are entrenched members of an unreasonable community, much like Goldman's zodiacal believers.)

(Are the beliefs of recently envatted brains reasonable in the current sense? Are the beliefs of native brains-in-vats reasonable? I imagine that the notion of reasonableness, even on the assumption that it is one employed by "the folk," is far too vague for these questions to have determinate answers. The notion of a reasonable person does not determinately express a single notion definable in terms of knowledge. It exhibits the "nonfactualism" that Field attaches to the more central evaluative conception of justification.

Indeed, perhaps it would be better to say that there is *no* notion of justification in the vicinity. In forming beliefs, one's goal should be knowledge.

Sometimes, one will form beliefs that fail to satisfy that goal, despite one's best efforts, and despite one not exhibiting any *general* tendency to form beliefs that do not constitute knowledge in unexceptional epistemic circumstances. And that is that. We do not have, and do not need, a notion of justification whose extension includes such beliefs that fail to meet the goal of knowledge whether or not it excludes those that succeed, any more than we need a notion of justification that encompasses but is distinct from the notion of blameless belief [in its secondary, knowledge-independent sense].)

The word 'justification' is perhaps connected with belief in common speech, not as a *property* of a belief, but in the notion of someone's justification *for* a belief. Such justifications can be adequate or inadequate; I contend that an adequate justification for a belief is one such that, if the belief were formed on its basis, it would constitute knowledge. A belief that has an adequate justification for an individual, then, is once again to be identified with knowledge. An inadequate justification is one that fails in its aim—it does not render that for which it is a justification known.[39]

1.3.6   Other Allegedly Justified Beliefs

As stated above, many epistemologists contend that there are justified beliefs other than the unknown unknown and known unknown, but just *which* beliefs those are is a matter of great dispute. Reliabilists, for example, contend that beliefs formed using reliable processes, processes of belief formation that result in true rather than false beliefs most of the time, are justified. Each reliabilist theory is of course considerably more complex and sophisticated in its details than this sketch portrays, but, whatever the details, beliefs that are justified according to a reliabilist theory that neither constitute knowledge nor are members of the unknown unknown and known unknown categories are not justified in any *intuitive* sense. This is not to say that they are *unjustified* in an intuitive sense; raw intuitions about justification, such as they are, are often silent on how to classify such beliefs. (Much of the goal of this chapter and the next is to reveal the implicit assumptions underlying our intuitions about justification and to undermine those intuitions by undermining those assumptions.)

Even more crudely, one might at first pass characterize reliabilism as stating that a belief is justified if and only if it is *probably* true given the manner in which it was formed. On such a characterization, those justified beliefs that do not constitute knowledge have some similarities to the known unknown beliefs, although there is one important dissimilarity. To be justified in a reliabilist sense, it is not required that the believer in any sense be *aware* that his belief is formed by a reliable process or that it is probably true.[40] However, it is hard to see how such an awareness that one's belief is probably true, but only *probably* true, could render one's belief unjustified if it would have been justified were one not so aware *unless* such awareness made one's belief blameworthy, which is not an epistemic notion that is in the spirit of externalist theories of justification *at all*. Consequently, if the known unknown beliefs are not justified, reliabilists about justification have some explaining to do.

(What is it to be a reliabilist *without* propounding or endorsing some particular reliabilist theory? There certainly appear to be a number of epistemologists who would claim to be reliabilists *in a general sense,* but I suggest that it is much less clear what that amounts to than what being an externalist amounts to [about knowledge or justification] without commitment to any particular externalist theory. *If* all it takes to be a reliabilist is to be an externalist about justified belief, a fallibilist in the sense that one holds that a belief can be unjustified while sharing all *internal* characteristics with beliefs of other possible or actual believers that *are* justified [one hence cannot easily become aware of the lack of justification], *then* I am a reliabilist, too.)

This is, however, a relatively minor quibble with reliabilism; it can no doubt be dealt with by exploiting the details of one's preferred reliabilist theory or by adding new details to one's definition. I will be arguing that neither the known unknown *nor* the unknown unknown beliefs are genuinely justified. If my arguments succeed, then the only intuitive cases of justified belief remaining will be beliefs that constitute knowledge. Should we immediately conclude that justification just is knowledge and leave it at that? I doubt that even those who accept my arguments will be happy to do so. The development of theories of justification (unlike much of the development of definitions of knowledge) does not in general proceed by testing a theory against intuition in the sense that a successful theory must rule all and only the intuitively justified beliefs justified by the lights of the theory. Indeed, if one's theory of justification is to serve at least partially as a theory of warrant, such accord with intuition is positively unwelcome since a solution to Gettier problems requires denying that the unknown unknown beliefs are warranted, as explained in section 1.3.1.

Many disputes arise because an opponent of a theory argues that a belief that is intuitively *unjustified* is justified according to the opposed theory.[41] But it is rarely held against a theory that it merely exceeds intuitive bounds, that it declares justified beliefs that are not clearly justified or unjustified in the light of pretheoretical intuition. "Spoils to the victor" in such cases, as David Lewis was fond of saying in other contexts. This is perhaps a suspicious way to proceed. If the development of a theory is in large part unconstrained by intuitions about concrete cases, disputes between competing theories are likely to be continued endlessly without movement toward a resolution, unless each side's decision to ignore the other and develop its theories in isolation counts as resolution. (I contend that the literature on justification, particularly in the rivalry between internalists and externalists, is an instance of the phenomenon.)

If intuition is not the proving ground of theories of justification, what is? The development of theories of justification tends to proceed, at least implicitly, by testing a theory against how well it conforms to one or more of the concepts of justification described above. The concern of most theories of justification, internalist or externalist, is primarily to define *evaluative* justification, when a belief is a good thing (or not a bad thing) from an epistemic point of view. The concern of most internalist theories of justification, and the concern of minority externalists such as Kornblith, is also to define *deontological* justification, what one should or should not believe. Even those philosophers who do not try to define justification *in general,* but merely the conditions under which beliefs of particular types are justified— testimonial beliefs or fundamental perceptual beliefs, for example—are very often driven not by intuitions about concrete cases, but by the desire to meet the abstract goals of evaluative or deontological justification. Which testimonial beliefs are a good thing from an epistemic point of view? Is one *entitled* to take testimony or the deliverances of one's senses at face value?

Many theories of justification, particularly internalist theories, also seek simultaneously to define blameless belief, just as many theories, particularly externalist theories, also seek to define warrant. These relatively abstract goals are rather removed from intuitions about the justificatory status of particular concrete beliefs, and, especially in combination with a failure clearly to distinguish the various concepts of justification (most importantly, the *secondary* senses of blameless belief and warrant described above from all the other concepts), a primary concern with satisfying such goals suits the pathology of theory development substantially unconstrained by intuition described above.

So, my overall argument that justification is knowledge proceeds in two stages, and the preliminary stage is complete. There is no good reason to think that either deontological or evaluative justification (or belief blameless by the lights of Reason alone) amounts to something distinct from knowledge *except* for the intuitiveness of taking the unknown unknown beliefs and/or the known unknown beliefs to be justified, although they do not constitute knowledge. And other supposed concepts of justified belief are either no such thing, such as belief that is blameless in the most general sense, or they are very peripheral compared to the others, such as reasonableness, or they are empty, as perhaps warrant is. Those claims are what I have argued for so far in describing my view, partially by contrast with more orthodox theories of justification. In the next chapter, I will present four arguments that neither the unknown unknown beliefs nor the known unknown beliefs are justified, and will seek to undermine further the intuitive basis for the claim that there is justification without knowledge, completing the overall argument that justification simply is knowledge.

In light of the overall argument, it is no objection to my view that some particular epistemological issue that I have perhaps not considered fully or at all *might require* a knowledge-independent notion of justified belief, since the argument, I contend, establishes that there is no such notion to be had (except for something like the knowledge-*dependent* reasonableness of section 1.3.5). Consequently, however much one imagines that *something* extra is needed for some purpose or other, what is demanded is that one provide some account of what justified belief might be given the argument that I make; we need more than an admission that one knows not what justified belief is but that it is not what one knows. If that burden of proof cannot be met, then it is in keeping with the view defended here that one try making do with nothing but knowledge alone (or some notion that can be defined in terms of knowledge). The third and fourth chapters of the book make the case that that approach works well for a number of central epistemological problems.

In later chapters, I will consider many times beliefs that are *intuitively* justified but that do not constitute knowledge, although my argument that such beliefs are not justified will be complete at the end of the first two chapters, and I hope that the reader's intuitions will be on the way to changing in the light of my arguments. (Intuitions are a good place to start epistemology, but they are subject to revision. I am in at least that much agreement with the practice of abandoning constraint by intuitions in the development of a theory of justification.) I nevertheless return to the known unknown and particularly the unknown unknown to contrast my views on matters such as testimony and inference with other views available to proponents of broader notions of justification, and to argue that such alternatives are incorrect for reasons quite independent of my identification of justification and knowledge. I will not, however, consider all the many beliefs that do not constitute knowledge and are not justified in any intuitive sense that various actual and possible theories of justification declare to be justified. There is no way to take into account all such theories, and, given the arguments of these two chapters, all such theories lack motivation in any case. Allegedly justified beliefs whose status as such is merely theory-driven will concern us no more.

Some epistemologists (such as Plantinga, as we saw in section 1.3.1) appeal extensively to the notion of *degrees* of justification, and such epistemologists might well appeal to the notion in response to some of my arguments. I will not be considering theories of justification that proceed along these lines either, for the simple reason that one must *first* establish that one has a coherent account of *fully* justified belief (and fully unjustified belief) before one is entitled to appeal to partially justified belief. And the first step is precisely what I am arguing cannot be reached if one does not identify justification and knowledge.[42]

2   The Arguments

2.1   Four Arguments

A view as unorthodox as mine demands more than a single argument: I offer four in this chapter, followed by a discussion of the most important objection to (three of) my arguments.[1] The four arguments stand alone; each is supposed to establish its conclusion without help from the others. Nevertheless, they also work together in demonstrating a number of diverse phenomena that are best explained by the hypothesis that justification is knowledge.

Everyone allows that many people have many unjustified beliefs, and everyone has some unjustified beliefs, but such beliefs appear to be far more prevalent on my view than on more orthodox views. In the third section, I argue that unjustified beliefs, although widespread, are not quite as common as they might appear to be on my view. That section also serves to undermine the intuitive support for the claim that there are justified beliefs that do not constitute knowledge in a more comprehensive fashion than the previous chapter did by arguing that there is a pervasive *loose* usage of the phrase 'justified belief' in which it is quite true that many intuitively justified beliefs that do not amount to knowledge are "justified." Strictly speaking, however, there are no such beliefs. This leads into a section on the paradox of the preface, the discussion of which illustrates what is correct and what is incorrect in internalist theories of justification. In the final section, I suggest that a functionalist view of knowledge is preferable to any traditional definition of the notion, and close by arguing that contextualist views of knowledge ascription are false.

2.1.1 The Assertion Argument

Philosophers including Peter Unger (1975), Michael Slote (1979), Keith DeRose (1996), and Timothy Williamson (2000) have argued on broadly similar grounds that one is not warranted in making an assertion that p unless one knows that p.[2] The notion of warrant involved is explicitly deontological for Williamson (and for Unger) who says that "one must: assert p only if one knows p" (Williamson 2000, 243), a norm—the knowledge rule—the following of which he takes to be constitutive of assertion. In this section I will review Williamson's main arguments, which are the most exhaustive of the four authors, for the claim that warranted assertion requires knowledge. I will then argue that the entailment from warranted assertability to knowledge is inexplicable unless there is a similar entailment from justified belief to knowledge. One must: believe p only if one knows p, a norm that is as constitutive of belief as Williamson's knowledge rule is of assertion.

I shall divide Williamson's arguments for his knowledge rule into three, further discussion and defense of which can, of course, be found in Williamson's text. The first states that the knowledge rule is required to explain why quasi-Moorean assertions of the form 'p and I don't know that p' are deeply unacceptable. Sentences of this form could clearly be *true;* the knowledge rule explains why they implicate something that clearly contradicts what is explicitly asserted. An assertion is presumed to obey the norms governing assertion. We assume, then, that the asserter knows the asserted conjunction, which entails that he knows the first conjunct, that is, that he knows that p, which is explicitly denied in the second conjunct.

The second argument is that lottery cases seem to show that evidential standards falling short of knowledge are not sufficient to warrant assertion. If one buys a lottery ticket, no matter how probable it is that one's ticket will lose, and no matter how aware one is of that probability, one is not warranted in asserting that one will not win. Almost everyone acknowledges that one does not *know* that one's ticket will lose; the knowledge rule, then, explains the unacceptability of the assertion that one will lose. The third argument simply appeals to the appropriateness (considerations of politeness and tact aside) of challenges and rebukes to assertions such as 'How do you know?' and 'You don't know that!'

Now, let us suppose (for the purposes of a *reductio ad absurdum*) that Andy has a justified true belief that p that does not amount to knowledge that p. (This is impossible on some views of justification, namely, those that take justification to be warrant in the *secondary* sense of section 1.3.1— whatever property [which true or false beliefs might have] that, combined with truth, renders a belief knowledge. I will extend the argument to such views below.) We might take 'p' to be a member of the unknown unknown beliefs, for example, that Andy is giving Bob a dollar bill, believed in the land of fake dollar bills, or a member of the known unknown beliefs, for example, that Andy's ticket will not win the lottery. By the knowledge rule, it is impermissible for Andy to assert that p to Bob, but let us suppose that Andy makes this unwarranted assertion and that Bob believes what he is told. Let us moreover suppose that both Andy's and Bob's beliefs that p are justified by whatever alleged standards of justification one cares to select (externalist or internalist, deontological or evaluative) falling short of knowledge consistent with the case.[3] For example, we might suppose that Andy formed his belief by a process that fairly reliably produces truths *if* a true belief could arise by such a process that was justified but did not constitute knowledge (reliabilists might differ on this point). We can suppose that Bob's reliance on Andy's testimony is similarly reliable. Indeed, we might suppose that Andy *only* utters truths in actual and a wide range of counterfactual circumstances, so that Bob's belief perhaps has an even higher degree of justification than Andy's, although he cannot know that p on the basis of Andy's testimony unless Andy knows that p.[4] We can also suppose that Andy's belief is impeccably justified by whatever internalist standards one likes consistent with his not knowing that p, and that Bob's reliance on Andy's testimony is similarly free of internalist blemish.

More generally, if there *is* a gap between justified true belief and knowledge, we can suppose that that gap is exemplified in the case of Andy and Bob; the details will vary wildly, of course, depending on the particular theory of justification we select. Andy has a justified true belief that p that does not constitute knowledge, and he asserts that p to Bob who has, we can suppose, the very best reasons for thinking—indeed, he knows—that Andy is expressing what is for him a justified belief.[5] Bob, then, has acquired a true belief that p that is justified by any number of standards that one likes consistent with it falling short of knowledge. Bob's belief violates none of his epistemic duties, and it lives up to primary epistemic goals; it is, we can further suppose, a *good thing* in numerous ways for Bob to believe that p. He will be healthier, wealthier, and wiser as a result. And yet, the knowledge rule tells us, Andy should not have asserted that *p*.

This is exceptionally puzzling. One of the main goals of making assertions, if not *the* main goal, is to transmit beliefs from one thinker to another.[6] If the beliefs so transmitted meet the primary standards governing good belief for both speaker and hearer—that is, they are justified in an evaluative sense—and meet standards of permissible belief (as noted previously, it is hard to imagine the former standards being met without the latter), it would be mysterious if the assertions transmitting the beliefs failed to meet the standards governing good assertion. On the contrary, the assertions in question have to meet the standards governing good assertion impeccably since they transmit impeccable beliefs. It is not, however, the knowledge rule that is at fault; the arguments of Williamson and others for that rule are good ones. It is our initial supposition that was at fault. There are no justified true beliefs falling short of knowledge, so Andy cannot have one. Assertions that transmit impeccable beliefs are impeccable assertions according to the knowledge rule since all impeccable beliefs constitute knowledge.

What, then, if there *are* no justified true beliefs that fail to constitute knowledge; what if the only workable notion of justification is a notion of warrant that in combination with truth suffices for knowledge? I suggest that my argument can be modified to retain its effectiveness, although it is perhaps a little diminished. (The modified argument also works as a supplementary argument that justification is knowledge for those who are not proponents of warrant.) We now must suppose that Andy transmits a warranted belief that falls short of knowledge to Bob, who satisfies all the other conditions specified above (for example, he knows that Andy is expressing a belief that is warranted for him). That is to say, Andy transmits a warranted *false* belief to Bob; Bob ends up with a warranted false belief in the same proposition in which Andy has a warranted false belief. Once again, we ask the question: how could an assertion that transmits a warranted belief from Andy to Bob be an unwarranted assertion when one of the main goals of assertion is precisely to transmit belief?[7] To which question it seems that there is an obvious answer: Andy told Bob something false, although his belief in it was warranted. Of course there was something wrong with his assertion.

The answer is a little too glib, however. Andy's and Bob's beliefs are also false, there is also something wrong with them, but they are warranted.

Why should the standards for warranted assertion be so much stricter than the standards for warranted belief when one of the main goals of assertion is to transmit belief? Once again, I suggest that they are not, and that is because a counterpart knowledge rule applies equally to belief.

One might respond that my characterization of the goal of assertion is simply mistaken. It is not one of the goals of assertion to transmit belief; in light of the knowledge rule, it is clearly to transmit knowledge. Indeed, one might go further and claim that Bob cannot himself acquire a warranted belief from Andy unless Andy expresses knowledge. No warranted false belief can transmit its warrant to another via testimony. If that is so, then the belief that Bob acquires will be as defective as Andy's assertion, and there is harmony between the standards of belief and assertion.

These defenses do not remove our initial puzzle, however. If a belief can be warranted despite being false, it is bizarre that an assertion conveying such a belief is unwarranted. Why do the main goals of assertion fail to encompass the conveying of such beliefs? Why is an assertion not doing its job when it conveys such a belief? It would add to our bafflement if Bob could not acquire a warranted belief from Andy's expression of a warranted false belief. Why would assertion not act as a conduit for warranted belief as well as knowledge proper? The best explanation of such phenomena would be that warranted belief just is knowledge: that is why Bob acquires a warranted belief only if Andy expresses knowledge, for only in those conditions is Andy's belief itself warranted (there being no such thing as warrant in the secondary sense of section 1.3.1, if it is supposed to be evaluative justification as well as a component of knowledge).

It will also do no good to claim that what is wrong with Andy's assertion, whether one considers the original case or the modified warranted false belief case, is that Andy potentially misleads Bob into thinking that he *does* know since that is implicated by his having made the assertion in the light of the knowledge rule. It is very strange that there should *be* any such implication if there are justified beliefs falling short of knowledge since it is hard to see how an assertion that transmitted such beliefs would be defective. One cannot appeal to the knowledge rule itself in trying to explain away the odd combination of justified beliefs that do not constitute knowledge and the knowledge rule; that is to ignore the oddity of the combination, not explain it away.

I will close this section with a new line of thought that bolsters my case that the knowledge rule is only explicable if justification is knowledge. The knowledge rule is arguably subject to exceptions since in some cases it is arguable that speakers regularly assert falsehoods to communicate truths. It is sometimes suggested that so-called restricted quantification is one such example; when I assert (falsely, it is suggested) that everyone has been told of the meeting, I might communicate the truth that everyone in my workplace has been told of the meeting.[8] If such a phenomenon occurs, it is surely pervasive, and we must suppose that such assertions are warranted. What is notable is that the falsehoods asserted in such situations would neither express the literal content of the speaker's belief, which would be the expanded counterpart truth, nor would they have any tendency to induce a belief in the falsehoods in the audience, who would also form a belief in the expanded counterpart truth. That is, these assertions do not induce unjustified beliefs in their audience (nor do they express unjustified beliefs of the speaker). This suggests that the knowledge rule governing assertions is perhaps an imperfect expression of the relation between belief and assertion. One should assert only what one justifiably believes when there is otherwise a risk of inducing unjustified beliefs in one's audience. If justification is knowledge, this generalization explains both the knowledge rule that governs most assertions and the possible exceptions described above. The counterpart to the knowledge rule governing belief is what is fundamental.[9]

2.1.2 The Lottery Argument

This argument builds on the work of Dana Nelkin (2000), who presents two versions of the lottery paradox, one concerning knowledge and the other justification, and argues that they should receive a solution that locates the flaw in each paradoxical argument in the same place (in fact, counterpart premises).[10] I will review the two paradoxes as Nelkin presents them, then review her reasons for faulting the premises that she does. Nelkin's uniform solution to the paradoxes involves denying that the belief that one's ticket will not win is justified. I will argue that Nelkin's explanation of why it is unjustified is incomplete at best. The best explanation, I will argue, is that justification is knowledge.

The Knowledge Paradox

1. Jim knows that his ticket t_1 will lose.

2. If Jim knows that his ticket t_1 will lose, then he knows that t_2 will lose, he knows that t_3 will lose . . . and he knows that $t_{1,000,000}$ will lose.

So,

3. Jim knows that t_1 will lose . . . and Jim knows that $t_{1,000,000}$ will lose. (1, 2)

4. Jim knows that either t_1 will not lose or t_2 will not lose . . . or $t_{1,000,000}$ will not lose.

5. Propositions of the following form comprise an inconsistent set: (a) p1 . . . (n) pn, (n + 1) not p1 or . . . not pn.

So,

6. Jim knows propositions that form an inconsistent set. (3, 4, 5)

7. It is not possible to know propositions that form an inconsistent set.

So,

8. (1), (2), (4), (5), or (7) is false.

(Nelkin 2000, 374, obvious typographical error corrected)

The Justification Paradox

1*. Jim could justifiably believe that his ticket t_1 will lose.[11]

2*. If Jim could justifiably believe that his ticket t_1 will lose, then he could justifiably believe that t_2 will lose, he could justifiably believe that t_3 will lose . . . and he could justifiably believe that $t_{1,000,000}$ will lose.

So,

3*. Jim could justifiably believe that t_1 will lose . . . and Jim could justifiably believe that $t_{1,000,000}$ will lose. (1*, 2*)

4*. Jim could justifiably believe that either t_1 will not lose or t_2 will not lose . . . or $t_{1,000,000}$ will not lose.

5*. Propositions of the following form comprise an inconsistent set: (a) p1 . . . (n) pn, (n + 1) not p1 or . . . not pn.

6*. Jim recognizes that the following propositions form an inconsistent set: (i) t_1 will lose . . . (n) $t_{1,000,000}$ will lose, either t_1 will not lose . . . or $t_{1,000,000}$ will not lose.

So,

7*. Jim could justifiably believe inconsistent things that he recognizes are inconsistent. (3*, 4*, 5*, 6*)

8*. One cannot justifiably believe things that one recognizes are inconsistent.

So,

9*. (1*), (2*), (4*), (5*), (6*), or (8*) is false.

(Nelkin 2000, 375, obvious typographical error corrected, and claims about what "it is rational for Jim to believe" replaced by claims about what he could justifiably believe)

Our conclusions below will apply whether the premises of the justification paradox are understood deontologically or evaluatively. (Premise (1*), for example, can be paraphrased as "it is permissible for Jim to believe that his ticket t_1 will lose" and premise (9*) as "One ought not believe things that one recognizes are inconsistent," or the notion of justification employed throughout can be understood in terms of the satisfaction of epistemic goals.)

Nelkin notes that almost everyone thinks that premise (1) is at fault in the knowledge version of the paradox; one simply does not know that one's ticket will lose however aware one is of the very small chance that it has of winning. She notes that the justification version of the paradox rarely inspires such a reaction, prompting unintuitive positions that block the transferral of justification from premises to conclusions of apparent paradigms of good inference. For example, Foley (1979) denies (8*) by denying the conjunction rule that belief in a conjunction is justified if belief in each conjunct is.[12] However, the difference between the solutions that have been offered to the two versions of the paradox is in part because both versions are rarely discussed together, yet it is a clear desideratum of a solution to one version that it can be applied to the other. However uncomfortable it is to deny the conjunction rule for justification, it is far harder to swallow the claim that it does not hold for knowledge, which a parallel solution to the knowledge paradox would require.[13] Denying premise (1) seems to be by far the best strategy with respect to the knowledge paradox, and Nelkin advocates denying (1*) on that basis. Indeed, it is hardly unintuitive to deny (1); the knowledge version of the paradox is not really a paradox at all, but simply an unsound argument. This does not undercut the force of Nelkin's point that the two unsound arguments ought to receive the same diagnosis, even if only one is a genuine paradox.

Of course, we need an explanation of why premise (1*) of the justification paradox is incorrect. I will review Nelkin's explanation below. My explanation is simple. Premise (1*) is false because it *is* premise (1); in a fundamental sense, the justification paradox just is the knowledge "paradox," and the solution to the paradox is to see that it is just the "paradox," which is nothing more than an unproblematically unsound argument. Justification is knowledge. Hence, to say that Jim could justifiably believe that his ticket t_1 will lose is to say that he could know that his ticket will lose—that he could know given just the grounds for belief that he already has, that if he were to believe, then he would know.[14] Premise (1*) is false because premise (1) is false since they express more or less the same proposition (ignoring the modal phrasing of (1*)). The identification of justification and knowledge receives support from the fact that it enables a parallel diagnosis of the knowledge paradox and the justification paradox.

Such support is weakened if there is some other viable explanation of why (1*) is false. Nelkin aims to provide just such a diagnosis.[15] First, she notes that many externalist theories of knowledge require that there be a "causal or explanatory" connection between the fact that p and the belief that p if that belief is to constitute knowledge (a connection that she endorses and for which she argues). This connection is lacking if one's belief that one's ticket will lose is based on merely probabilistic grounds—it is missing in the lottery case, and that is why one does not know that one's ticket will lose. Second, she postulates that justification requires an internalized version of the causal or explanatory connection that knowledge requires (which is not to say that that is *all* that justification requires). To be justified in believing that p, the believer must be able to "suppose that there is . . . a causal or . . . explanatory connection between one's belief and its object" (Nelkin 2000, 397), and Jim cannot see that there is any such connection for his belief that his ticket will lose—indeed, he can see that there is no such connection. Nelkin notes that the believer's supposition that there is a causal or explanatory connection between his belief that p and the fact that p must itself be justified if that supposition is to render the belief that p justified.[16]

I do not see that Nelkin's introduction of causal and explanatory relations is of any utility except insofar as it explains why Jim does not know that his ticket will lose (a utility that Nelkin explicitly takes it to have). If we take it for granted that Jim does not know that for *whatever* reason, it seems that talk of causal and explanatory relations adds nothing to Nelkin's account of why Jim's belief would not be justified. The relevance that Jim's inability to see such connections has to his lack of justification is just that it renders Jim unable to postulate justifiably that he *knows* that his ticket will lose, the connections in question being precisely those that are necessary for a belief to constitute knowledge. So, what Nelkin's account of why (1*) is false boils down to is that a belief that *p* is not justified unless the believer justifiably believes (or *could* justifiably believe or would justifiably believe upon reflection) that he knows that *p*. Now, Nelkin does not explain *why* justified belief should require justifiably believing (at least on reflection) that one knows that *p*. Indeed, since she stresses that Jim can "see" (her term) that his belief does *not* have the appropriate causal or explanatory connections to its object, all she is really doing is pointing out that Jim is in a position to know that he does not know that his ticket will lose. That is, she is not explaining why premise (1*) is false, but simply pointing out that lottery beliefs belong to that category of allegedly justified beliefs we have been calling the known unknown beliefs. Nelkin is doing little beyond baldly asserting that such beliefs are not justified.[17] Her "explanation" is the start of a genuine explanation of the falsity of (1*), however. The reason *knowledge* is at the heart of her characterization of justification is that justification just *is* knowledge, and the lottery beliefs are hence unjustified since they do not constitute knowledge.

(What might a proponent of justification as warrant say in response to the lottery paradox? Since what is characteristic about warrant is that a warranted true belief is supposed necessarily to be knowledge, the only tenable strategy is to endorse Nelkin's claim and my own that (1*) is false. If one's belief that one's ticket will lose is warranted, then, provided one's ticket actually does lose, one knows that one's ticket will lose; this is not so, hence we must conclude that one's belief that one's ticket will lose is not warranted. The same reasoning renders the rest of the class of known unknown, allegedly justified beliefs unwarranted, unless one wants to claim that only the false examples are warranted! [That having been said, I am not at all sure how many popular accounts of warrant avoid a commitment to our knowing that our tickets will lose. A general strategy of forming such probabilistically based beliefs certainly reliably yields truths, for example.])[18]

2.1.3 The Modesty Argument

This argument concludes that there are no known unknown justified beliefs. It is the only argument whose conclusion concerns only *some* of the allegedly justified beliefs. Although my other arguments make use of a proper subset of the allegedly justified beliefs (e.g., the lottery argument), their conclusions are general: the only justified beliefs are those that constitute knowledge.

If the belief that p is one of the known unknown beliefs, then, by definition, one is generally in a position to know that one does not know that p. I am not, of course, in any way claiming that one is infallible in determining that one does not know such a proposition. No doubt thinkers fairly often take themselves to know theories that are false or, at best, lacking sufficient support to constitute knowledge. No doubt thinkers often take themselves to know propositions that at best they know to be probable. Most such thinkers (at least) have some unjustified beliefs, however—their estimations of the extent of their knowledge. I am arguing that those thinkers and others who do not explicitly overestimate what they know (in a sense, any belief that falls short of knowledge implicitly overestimates the extent of one's knowledge on my view) but still have beliefs in the known unknown class are unjustified in *those* beliefs, rather than their beliefs about the extent of their knowledge.

The skeleton of the argument is suggested by Nelkin in her attempt to explain away the appeal of the claim that Jim is justified in thinking that his lottery ticket will lose ('the lottery claim'):

Strongly associated with the appeal of [the lottery claim] is the conviction that Jim should not make plans contingent on his winning the lottery, and, in fact, that he should make plans based on the assumption that he is not going to win. Similarly, we think that he should not "get his hopes up," that he should not devote excessive energy to creating mental images of his winning, and that [perhaps] he should not buy a lottery ticket. . . . In fact, I believe that the appeal of [the lottery claim] derives largely from the fact that Jim's belief that he will lose rationalizes all of these behaviors that we find rational and normative for Jim.

But . . . compatible with the falsity of [the lottery claim] is the truth of

1**. Jim is [justified] in believing that he will very probably lose.

All of the behaviors just mentioned (making plans on the assumption that he will lose, not getting his hopes up, and so on) are sufficiently rationalized by Jim's belief that he will very probably lose. (Nelkin 2000, 400)

Explicitly probabilistic beliefs such as that described in (1**) are justified on anyone's view, including my own, since they constitute knowledge in the relevant cases. Nelkin suggests that these beliefs are at least as good a guide to behavior as their bolder, nonprobabilistic counterparts from a third-person perspective *and*, more importantly, from a first-person perspective. One gains nothing—no motive for rational action, and no benefits thereof— from believing immodestly that one will lose the lottery that one does not gain from believing modestly that one will very likely lose the lottery.

This is not to say that believing that one is very likely to lose the lottery and believing that one will lose the lottery do not differ at all in their (potential) effects on a believer's behavior. Believing categorically that one will lose the lottery will lead to the kind of behavior that is associated with greater confidence than its probabilistic counterpart. But such behavior will be the behavior of the irrationally overconfident. Indeed, if one believes categorically that one's ticket will lose the lottery, one invites the question that is often posed rhetorically to illustrate that one does not *know* that one's ticket will lose. If one believes categorically that one's ticket will lose, why did one buy the ticket in the first place? (That this does seem like an appropriate question is nicely explained by my view that belief *aims* at knowledge, that a belief is only properly held when it constitutes knowledge.)[19]

(None of the foregoing should be taken to suggest that it is always *easy* or even *possible* to say whether someone categorically believes a proposition *p* or merely believes that it is probable that *p*. Just which proposition a believer believes is subject to the phenomenon of vagueness. Whether indeterminacy is merely epistemic or genuinely metaphysical in this realm [a subject of much dispute (see Williamson 1994)], it can be indeterminate whether someone believes that *p* or merely believes that it is extremely likely that *p*. This is perhaps most often the case when it comes to propositions that a believer has not explicitly considered and merely believes whatever it is that he believes *implicitly* [a subject we will return to briefly in section 3.2].

Even if it is determinate just which proposition someone bears an attitude to in some case, it might be indeterminate which attitude he bears to it—does a believer *believe* that *p* or merely *suspect* that *p*?)

So much for the explicitly probabilistic subdivision of the known unknown beliefs—what about what we might term the "theoretical" subdivision, beliefs in theories that are best supported by the evidence, but not so well supported that one knows them to be true? What is the modest thing to believe that will gain one all the advantages as a guide to rational action that a brasher belief would? Simply that the evidence supports one theory over the others (and to such-and-such a degree, insofar as one can make such a claim). Believing in the theory outright will, once again, be an instance of irrational overconfidence and invites a question similar to one that arose in the explicitly probabilistic case, at least for "active" proponents of a theory rather than those who believe the theory because of, say, what they read in the newspaper. If one categorically believes the theory to be true, why is one still investigating its truth—gathering further evidence (if one is a scientist concerned with an empirical theory), looking for new arguments (if one is a philosopher concerned with a philosophical theory), and so on?

Why not be maximally modest, one might ask? Do not *ever* believe that a theory is true; simply believe that the evidence supports (or *appears* to support?) it more or less well even if one does know it to be true—or would if one so believed. Never believe that one has lost the lottery, simply that it is very likely that one did, even when one watched the draw take place and knows that one lost (or would if one so believed). Indeed, never believe that one has hands, simply that it seems to be so. Does not our previous discussion lead to an endorsement of this absurd (and, no doubt, psychologically impossible) cognitive behavior?

It does not. The absence or presence of knowledge makes the difference between rational and irrational belief formation. The vast majority of discussions of irrational belief and irrational believers focus on beliefs that believers form that they should not. Some irrational believers qualify as such because of the beliefs that they *fail* to form, however. Some nonphilosophical skeptics (whose skepticism is restricted to specific areas of enquiry) are too skeptical. They should form beliefs that they do not form. Often (at least), they should form those beliefs because the nonskeptics who believe the contested propositions *know* them to be true and on the same grounds that the skeptic himself possesses.

Alternatively, consider someone suffering from an obsessive-compulsive disorder who just will not stop washing his hands. He does not think that they are clean, but he has such strong grounds for thinking that his hands are clean that if he were only to believe, he would know.[20] He *might* further believe that his hands are not clean, an irrational belief of an orthodox kind. But even if he were *agnostic* about the state of his hands, his handwashing would be irrational because motivated by an irrational *lack* of belief. (From the point of view of desire or goal satisfaction, his behavior is apparently unobjectionable—he does not believe that his hands are clean, and he wants them to be clean, so he is washing them.) The maximally modest believer would suffer from the same kind of irrationality—he refuses to believe what he is in a position to know. Moreover, restricting oneself *per impossibile* to believing merely that one *seems* to have hands would, I suppose, result in behavior characteristic of cognitive underconfidence. Would one attempt to block the rock hurtling toward one's head rather than throw oneself on one's back if one merely believed that one seemed to have hands?

The rational refrain from a belief that *p* upon considering possible situations in which not-*p* that they do not know not to obtain only if their not having ruled out those possibilities prevents them from knowing that *p*. Other possibilities are "properly ignored" by the rational (and, *pace* contextualism, which possibilities these are does not depend on the context in which knowledge is ascribed—or so I will argue in section 2.5.4).[21] The pusillanimous, who refrain from forming or who abandon a belief that *p* simply because there are possible situations that they have not "ruled out" in which not-*p* *although those situations would be properly ignored,* are as irrational as the compulsive handwasher. They would know if only they would believe.[22]

An optimal believer, whose beliefs are precisely as modest as is necessary to produce optimal behavior, who is neither overconfident nor underconfident in belief or subsequent action, is one who restricts his beliefs to what he knows. Such belief accords with primary epistemic goals, among which is, arguably, the optimal guidance of action—it is, then, justified in an evaluative sense. Being an epistemic ideal, such modesty accords well with a Kornblithian understanding of deontological justification; one ought to be ideally modest, which requires believing only what one knows. (And avoiding the knowledge-shy failure to form beliefs noted above. There is at least one positive epistemic obligation: if one would know that p were one to believe that p simply in virtue of so believing, one ought to believe that p.)[23]

2.1.4   The Posterior Evaluation Argument

If a belief that p is one that would be justified were one to form it, and it is in one's interest to have a belief in whether or not p, and one is capable of forming such a belief, then, in some intuitive sense, one should believe that p, although that 'should' is not purely a 'should' of epistemic obligation. It is rather a 'should' generated by prudential considerations of self-interest interacting with the epistemic goals that determine an evaluative notion of justification.[24] This claim is clearly true if we read 'would be justified' as 'would constitute knowledge'. I will argue that it is not true on any more expansive conception of evaluative justification that incorporates the unknown unknown class of beliefs, casting doubt on such conceptions. Whatever justification is, it is surely *valuable,* even if it is just one of several epistemic values. If there can be justification without knowledge, when knowledge is absent, but justification is present, something of value remains, at least if no factor *independent* of knowledge is present to remove the value of justification—a factor, that is, that might or might not be present when knowledge is absent. The situation described below is explicitly constructed to contain no such factor. The mere absence of knowledge cannot remove the value that justification has—unless, of course, justification is knowledge. The opening claim that one should in *a* sense believe that p in the specified conditions is compatible with there being other senses in which one should *not* believe that p, or even other senses in which one should believe that not-p. There are beliefs that certain individuals should not form in an important sense because the beliefs would be dangerous, upsetting, or even lethal—even if they would constitute *knowledge* if the individuals were to form them. I stipulate that the situation described below is not disposed to produce such beliefs. (As noted in section 1.3.1, no members of the class of unknown unknown beliefs are warranted in Plantinga's sense—not even the false ones should there be any, which of course there will not be if we take warrant in its *primary* sense in which it *is* knowledge—and hence the argument of this section is not an argument against any notion of warrant.)

Suppose that one has never driven a Ford, and one wants to. We might even suppose that there is some financial (or romantic, or whatever) advantage to one's doing so. And let us suppose that one has plenty of evidence that one has a (particular) colleague who has a Ford, and one knows that all of one's colleagues would let one drive their cars. However, that evidence is misleading. As in the famous Gettier case, one does have a colleague who owns a Ford, but it is not the colleague that one's misleading evidence indicates owns a Ford. Were one to form a belief on the basis of one's evidence that one has a colleague who owns a Ford, that belief would be true. Let us suppose further that it would be justified despite not constituting knowledge.

However, one fails to notice the apparent implications of one's evidence. One fails to form any belief on the basis of that evidence, and so does not come to the justified conclusion that one has a colleague who owns a Ford. Some time later, one realizes that one previously failed to realize the apparent implications of one's evidence, and one is aware that had one done so, one would have formed the belief that one had a colleague who owned a Ford. Further information has since come to light concerning the misleading nature of one's former evidence, however, and one is now aware that the belief that one would have formed would have failed to constitute knowledge despite being true. At that later time, then, one does know that one had a colleague who owned a Ford, although, let us suppose, it is now too late to garner the benefits that would have accrued to one had one believed earlier that one had such a colleague. Is there an intuitive sense in which one will now judge that one should then have formed the belief that one had a colleague who owned a Ford—an allegedly justified, true belief? Clearly, there is. That belief would have been true.[25] So one should have formed it. However, we can say exactly the same about a similar situation in which one has no evidence whatsoever that one has a colleague who owns a Ford, although in fact one has such a colleague. There is an intuitive sense in which one should have formed the belief that one had such a colleague despite the fact that such a belief would have been unjustified by anyone's lights. Such a belief would have been true.

Consider also a situation that is similar except insofar as one's very good evidence that one has a colleague who owns a Ford is *not* misleading; it is quite sufficient for its possessor to gain knowledge that he has a colleague who drives a Ford (the very colleague to whom the evidence points), provided he forms that belief. Which, once again, one fails to do. Evaluating one's former cognitive situation after the fact, is there an intuitive sense in which one should have formed the belief *apart* from the consideration that it would have been true? I contend that there is: one should have *known* that one had a colleague who owned a Ford, and this is to say, in the case at hand, that one has let oneself down, doxastically speaking, in a way that goes beyond having merely failed to form a true belief (for which one could not coherently blame oneself, the beneficial consequences notwithstanding).[26]

So, in one case there is an intuitive (but nonepistemic) sense in which one should have formed the belief that one had a colleague who owned a Ford because it would have been true, and in a different case there is a different intuitive sense (one partially epistemic) in which one should have formed that belief because it would have constituted knowledge. What we lack, I claim, is the intermediate case. When one could have formed an allegedly justified, true belief that one had a colleague who owned a Ford, which fell short of knowledge, but one failed to do so, there is no intuitive sense in which one should have done so beyond the nonepistemic sense in which one should have done so because it would have been true (and beneficial). We should expect there to be such a sense, a sense in which one should have formed a justified belief on the question of whether or not one had a colleague who owned a Ford, given that it is in one's interest to do so and that one was capable of so doing. The absence of the intermediate case is explicable if the sense in which one should have formed a justified belief on the matter in question just *is* the sense in which one should have known that one had a colleague who owned a Ford since justification is knowledge. A similar case can be made for any belief in the unknown unknown class of allegedly justified beliefs; none of them is genuinely justified.

2.2 The Main Objection

How one responds to objections to one's view and to one's arguments for one's view clarifies the view and the arguments for the view themselves, particularly when one's view is as unorthodox as my own. Consequently, I have explained many objections and my responses to them in the course of laying out my view and my arguments. One objection is so potentially devastating that it deserves separate treatment. If successful, the objection demolishes three of my four arguments; all but the posterior evaluation argument, which is arguably the least intuitively compelling of my arguments in any case. A view as unorthodox as mine demands more than a single argument. In this section I will explain the main objection to my arguments, and how it threatens to defeat three of them. I will then argue that the main objection is unsuccessful.

The main objection is very similar to an objection that Williamson discusses to his knowledge rule for assertion; it is, in a sense, an upgraded version of that objection that aims to avoid one of his counterobjections. I will argue that his counterobjection can also be upgraded to render the objection powerless once more. The objection is that a weaker norm governing assertion will account for the phenomena that Williamson cites in support of his knowledge rule. That rule is (Williamson 2000, 261):

(The RBK rule) One must: assert p only if one rationally believes that one knows p.

The RBK rule accounts for the quasi-Moorean phenomena. One cannot assert a sentence of the form 'p and I do not know p' since if such an assertion were correct, one would rationally believe both that one knows p and that one knows that one does not know p. If one rationally believes that one knows that one does not know p, then one rationally believes that one does not know p since knowledge entails truth and one knows that. So one rationally believes that one knows p and that one does not know p. That is impossible; the quasi-Moorean assertion is unwarranted on the RBK rule. The RBK rule also accounts for the fact that lottery assertions are unwarranted. One cannot assert that one has not won the lottery since one cannot rationally believe that one knows that one has not won the lottery. The rule also explains why 'How do you know?' and related statements are appropriate challenges to many assertions; a challenged asserter should be able to explain how he rationally believes that he knows what he asserted, which is to explain *ceteris paribus* how he knows what he asserted if the asserter actually does know what he asserted.

The first of Williamson's objections to the RBK rule is, fundamentally, that it makes assertions that express false unknown unknown beliefs warranted:

Suppose that I rationally believe myself to know that there is snow outside; in fact, there is no snow outside . . . yet something is wrong with my assertion; [the RBK account does not imply that there is]. [It] can allow that there is something wrong with my belief that I know that there is snow outside. . . . The [RBK account] lacks the resources to explain why we regard the false assertion itself, not just the asserter, as faulty. (Williamson 2000, 262)

The defender of the RBK account (we will stick with the name only temporarily) should say, I think, that this is not a *consequence* of his view— it *is* his view. The view is that it is not just assertions that express knowledge that are warranted, but also assertions that express any unknown unknown belief, whether true or false. Indeed, one does not know that one does not know that *p* (even upon minimal reflection) if one has an unknown unknown justified belief that *p* by definition; perhaps if one believed that one did *not* know that *p*, then one would not be justified in believing *p*.[27] That does not require that one believe that one does know that *p*. One might not have considered the matter, and one's belief and any assertion that expresses it is not *ipso facto* unwarranted. It is time to upgrade the RBK rule:

(The J rule) One must: assert *p* only if one has a justified belief that *p*.

Justified beliefs are those that constitute knowledge, together with the unknown unknown beliefs. The known unknown beliefs are simply not justified; that is the conclusion that we should draw from the assertion phenomena that Williamson uses to argue for the knowledge rule, which the upgraded J rule explains as well as the RBK rule, and in the same way. If one has a justified belief that *p*, then one cannot also have a justified belief that one does not know that *p*. The unknown unknown beliefs are would-be knowledge; in unexceptional circumstances, where one does not suffer from bad luck in one's external environment, one would know what one justifiably believes. Clearly one cannot both know that *p* and know that one does not know that *p*, and neither could one have done so but for exceptional bad luck. The quasi-Moorean phenomena are explained by the J rule. Lottery beliefs are not justified, so neither are assertions that express such beliefs.

If one has an unknown unknown, justified belief that *p*, since one would not know that one did not know that *p*, one will, upon reflection at least, believe that one does know that *p*; if one does not, either one would not have been justified in one's belief in the first place, or one would cease to be so upon reflection. Otherwise, it is hard to see how one would have known that

p but for exceptional bad luck in one's external environment. Consequently, the 'How do you know?' challenge to a warranted assertion is explicable even for those warranted assertions that express unknown unknown beliefs rather than knowledge.[28]

The J rule does indeed imply that certain false assertions are warranted, and Williamson claims that falsity is a defect in an assertion over and above the defect that it is in any belief that an assertion expresses. I find that claim considerably less intuitive than his related claim that the flagrant irrationality of an assertion is a defect over and above the defect that it is in a flagrantly irrational belief so expressed—a claim that he makes to dispatch the weaker BK rule that one must assert only what one believes that one knows (rationally or irrationally). Besides, falsity is not a defect in a belief in the sense that it renders the belief unjustified on the *standard* view of justification; it would be puzzling if falsity rendered an assertive expression of a justified belief unjustified. (Of course, it does no such thing on my view: a false belief is unjustified *per se* since it does not constitute knowledge.)

A second objection to the RBK rule that Williamson makes is that the knowledge rule provides a *simpler* account of warranted assertion than the RBK rule, and so the burden of proof is on the proponent of the RBK rule to refute the account based on the knowledge rule. It is here that upgrading the RBK rule to the J rule pays off. The RBK rule is indeed more complex than the knowledge rule as its three-letter acronym clearly reveals. The J rule, on the other hand, dispenses with the B and the K components of the RBK rule.[29] It is not obviously any more complex than the K rule, and so no account of warranted assertion based upon it clearly has the burden of proof.

I will argue that Williamson's complexity argument against an RBK account has a counterpart that will defeat an account based on the J rule. Before giving the counterpart argument, let us see how a proponent of the J rule can defeat three of my arguments. It is obvious how he can defeat the assertion argument. That Williamson's knowledge rule governs assertion was a premise of that argument; if it is rather the J rule that governs assertion, then that premise is false.

It is almost truistic to say that the J rule (or a close counterpart) is as much a rule that governs warranted belief as warranted assertion. One must not believe that p unless one is justified in so doing. The rule has some nontruistic bite when its proponent adds that it is only the unknown unknown beliefs, along with those beliefs that constitute knowledge, that are justified; the known unknown are unjustified. Let us call the relevant notion of justification 'U-justification'. The modesty argument concludes that the known unknown beliefs are not justified. It is hence not a problem for the view that a belief is justified if and only if it is U-justified. As Nelkin herself in effect argues, we can give uniform solutions to the knowledge and justification versions of the lottery paradox by denying that known unknown beliefs, such as beliefs that one will not win the lottery, are justified; *why* they are unjustified is a further question to which the proponent of U-justification need not supply an answer. The tenability of his view does not obviously hang upon the provision of an answer.

In any case, perhaps pointing out that one can know that one does not know that one will not win the lottery is enough of an answer. I *do* have an explanation of why the lottery belief is unjustified: justification is knowledge. Is that a better explanation than: justification is U-justification? I suggest that it is, *especially* in light of the resurrection of Williamson's complexity argument below. Without that resurrection, perhaps the proponent of U-justification could *half*-defeat the lottery argument. A full defeat—the provision of an equally compelling response to both versions of the lottery paradox—would require an explanation of why justification is U-justification.

Now for the resurrection of Williamson's complexity argument. The J rule is, in fact, more complex than the knowledge rule because of the considerations of section 1.2.1. U-justification is more complex than knowledge since the concept of U-justification is parasitic upon that of knowledge. A U-justified belief is a belief that constitutes knowledge or a belief that would have done so but for bad luck in the believer's external environment. At the very least, the burden of proof is shifted back to the proponent of the J rule. He must show that U-justification is in fact at least as primitive a concept as the concept of knowledge rather than one that we understand as a disjunction of knowledge and would-be knowledge.[30]

2.3   The Bit Where You Take It Back, Part II

Having completed exposition of my arguments that there is no distinction between justification and knowledge, I now turn to undermining further the intuitive support that the distinction has. On anyone's view, people form a lot of unjustified beliefs. On my view, they do so even more commonly than on perhaps any view other than a philosophical skeptic's. In this section, I want to suggest that unjustified beliefs, although common on my view, are not quite as common as one might suppose since belief—or at least belief within the known unknown class of allegedly justified beliefs—is less common than one might suppose. Further, in a loose sense of 'justified belief', those in possession of unknown unknown beliefs that p can be said to have a justified belief that p. Nevertheless, strictly speaking, justification is knowledge. I will also reconsider internalism and *its* intuitive support by arguing that something like internalism is correct, loosely speaking—but only loosely speaking.

Utterances of the form 'I believe that p' and similar forms ('I think that p', 'p, I believe', 'I think so', etc.) often, I suggest, do not express belief in the proposition that p. They express, rather, a belief that p is probable (more likely than not, perhaps). Consider a stranger who asks one where the post office is. One does not know, but has a vague idea that it is a mile to the right. Consequently, one says 'I believe that it is a mile down that way'. This is a perfectly proper utterance; I suggest that it is also not literally true. One does not believe categorically that the post office is a mile to the right; one believes that it is more likely there than not. Ironically, a sentence of the form 'I believe that p' is sometimes used to convey precisely that one does *not* believe that p, strictly speaking.[31] Even if I make an explicitly probabilistic self-ascription of belief, such as 'I believe that it is more likely than not that there are mice in the basement', it is entirely proper to report my belief without a probabilistic modifier—'He thinks that there are mice in the basement'. (Contrast with the unacceptability of reporting my assertion 'There are mice in the basement, more likely than not' with 'He says that there are mice in the basement'.) Third-person belief ascriptions need not attribute belief in the proposition that an overly literal interpretation would suggest any more than their first-person counterparts.

If you say that there is a $10 dollar bill in your hand, but it is in fact a counterfeit, I have argued that the belief that you express is unjustified, although blameless (except by the light of Reason alone). On the other hand, if you say that you think that it is going to rain, and you do so because of the ominous clouds in the sky, I claim that there is nothing wrong with the belief that prompts your statement—it is justified. But it is not, strictly speaking, the belief that it is going to rain—it is the belief that it probably will, which constitutes knowledge. Since the qualified beliefs, which I suggest apparently bolder ascriptions of belief in fact express, do, in general, constitute knowledge for their holders, unjustified belief is a lot less common than an overly literal understanding of belief ascriptions would indicate. Scientific theories provide another illustration. I take it that 'It is believed that birds are descended from dinosaurs' is a perfectly proper statement (or, if it is not, it is down to my ignorance of the debate over the relation between birds and dinosaurs). This is so even if *no one* literally believes that birds are descended from dinosaurs, but the strongest view that anyone holds is that they probably did, or that the available evidence supports that theory better than any rival theory, or some such. (Perhaps phenomena like these prompt talk among some philosophers of theory *acceptance* in science rather than belief therein, although some such philosophers seem to take acceptance to be less easily reducible to belief than a notion of acceptance based on the considerations above.)[32]

What goes for the term 'belief' goes for any qualification of it—'justified belief', for instance. Just as 'belief that *p*' is loosely used to denote both belief that *p strictly speaking* and belief that *probably p*, 'justified belief that *p*' is loosely used to denote both justified belief that *p* strictly speaking and justified belief that probably *p*. This is a usage beyond reproach on many occasions for philosophers and nonphilosophers alike. Indeed, I suggest that the usage is *always* beyond reproach for lawmakers, for example.[33]

But epistemologists should take care to speak strictly about belief. A failure to do so is responsible, I contend, for much confusion in epistemology. As stated in section 1.3.2, many philosophers find *internalism* very intuitive. Loose talk about justified belief is responsible for a lot of the intuitive basis of internalism.[34] As explained in section 1.2.2, what is probable for one depends very heavily on one's background knowledge, and what one thinker justifiably believes—that is, knows—to be probable another thinker justifiably believes—that is, knows—to be improbable. Probability (at least in the sense relevant to us) is, to that extent, subjective. If one uses 'justified belief that *p*' indiscriminately to denote both justified belief that *p* and mere justified belief that probably *p*, it will seem nearly incontestable that justified belief is as subjective as probability actually is—and externalism in all its varieties will seem incompatible with this obvious fact.[35] Closely tailoring the reliability of a belief-forming process to the believer's background beliefs, for example, will just seem like an epicycle to save a theory, reliabilism, that is wrong in spirit—if it can succeed at all, it will merely turn externalist lead into internalist gold while retaining an epicyclical leaden expression.[36] But, strictly speaking, no one can have a justified belief that not-p if another has a justified belief that p.[37] If one knows that p, another cannot know that not-p. But one subject can know (merely) that probably p and another know (merely) that probably not-p. (The first subject cannot, however, be said to know that p *period*, and neither can the second be described correctly as 'knowing that not-p'. That one *can* use 'belief' and hence 'justified belief' in the loose sense described above but *not* 'know' has no doubt prevented the view that justification and knowledge are one and the same from receiving more consideration.) Justification is not subjective in the relevant sense, but probability is—justified belief appears to inherit the subjectivity of probability only because one uses the phrase 'justified belief that p' loosely to refer to both justified belief that p and to what is, strictly speaking, mere justified belief that probably p. Loosely speaking, internalism about "justified belief" is both correct and a *consequence* of my own views—it is entirely compatible with the claim that justification is knowledge.

In fact, nothing has changed from our starting point of the intuitive cases of justified belief that do not amount to knowledge, *loosely speaking*. Those believers who have known unknown, allegedly justified beliefs *do* have justified beliefs that *probably p* for some proposition p, since that is precisely the limit of their knowledge, and those believers can be loosely said simply to believe justifiably that p. Many of those believers who *appeared* to have the stronger unjustified categorical beliefs that p, strictly speaking, have no such beliefs, although they can be said to have them, loosely speaking. Unknown unknown beliefs are unjustified, but there are justified beliefs in the vicinity. The possessor of the counterfeit bill knows that he *probably* has a $10 bill; the observer in the land of fake barns, whether he sees a real barn or not, knows that there is *probably* a barn before him; the possessor of misleading evidence that he has a particular colleague who owns a Ford knows that he *probably* has a colleague who owns a Ford. The possessor of the counterfeit bill hence has a justified belief that he *probably* has a $10 bill (and his counterparts recalled above have counterpart justified beliefs), and so he can, loosely speaking, be said to have a justified belief that he has a $10 bill. The identification of justification and knowledge is, loosely speaking, entirely compatible with our intuitions about believers that lack knowledge and have justified beliefs notwithstanding. Loosely speaking, those who have an unknown unknown belief that p and those who have a known unknown belief that p do indeed have a justified belief that p. But, strictly speaking, their belief that p is unjustified and it is their belief that probably p that is justified in both cases since it constitutes knowledge, and it is the latter belief that we correctly call justified when we speak loosely. That S believes that p *entails* that S believes that probably p, and the latter belief can amount to knowledge even if the former does not.[38]

If one *could* use 'know' as loosely as one can use 'believe', one who had an unknown unknown belief that p, whether true *or false,* could, loosely speaking, be said to know that p since he does know that probably p. Gettier cases would intuitively illustrate knowledge as well as justified belief, and it would not be intuitive that knowledge, loosely speaking, entails truth. This constitutes pretty strong evidence that one cannot so use 'know'. That one can use 'justified belief that p' loosely for what is, strictly speaking, justified belief that probably p is, I suggest, a large part of the intuitive basis of the claim that there are justified beliefs that do not constitute knowledge; that, together with a conflation of justified belief proper, blameless belief (in its secondary, most general sense), and what I earlier quasi-technically dubbed 'reasonable belief' (section 1.3.5), exhausts the intuitive appeal of the claim.[39]

Illegitimate appropriation of intuitive support by internalism is far from the most extreme example of confusion resulting from the loose usage of 'justified belief'. To see a more extreme example, we must consider the lottery paradox once more and its illegitimate companion, the paradox of the preface.[40]

2.4   The "Paradox" of the Preface

It is often claimed that any solution to the lottery paradox should yield a solution to the paradox of the preface, and vice versa.[41] It is easy to see why if 'justified belief that p' is used loosely to denote both justified belief that p in the strict sense and mere justified belief that probably p. If one draws no distinction between categorical beliefs and their probabilistic counterparts, *of course* I am justified in believing that my lottery ticket will not win. And *of course* if I am justified in believing that of my own ticket t_1, I am justified in believing of any other ticket t_i that it will not win. And yet I am clearly not justified in believing that (t_1 will not win & t_2 will not win & . . . & $t_{1,000,000}$ will not win), which follows by conjunction introduction from what I am justified in believing. So that *must* be the solution to the paradox—we have to deny that justified belief is closed under conjunction.

Continuing to use 'justified belief' loosely, the paradox of the preface looks very similar indeed to the lottery paradox—we should surely expect a uniform solution. Many books contain many unjustified statements that express unjustified beliefs—but not all books are like that. Many books are written sufficiently meticulously that the author is justified in everything he says and in the beliefs that his statements express; *a fortiori*, this is possible. Still, all but the most arrogant, meticulous authors will believe that they have made some errors—and they will be justified in believing that at least one of their statements and their corresponding beliefs is false.[42] So, the story goes, the meticulous author justifiably believes p_i where 'i' indexes in succession each of the propositions that he expresses in his book, and yet he justifiably believes not-(p_1 & . . . & p_n)—*a fortiori*, he cannot justifiably believe (p_1 & . . . & p_n). The solution here is as obvious as with the lottery paradox. Justification is not closed under conjunction. From the fact that one has a justified belief that p and a justified belief that q, it does not follow that one has or could have a justified belief that p & q.

And this all really is obvious if one uses 'justified belief' loosely—it is obvious that "justified belief" is not closed under conjunction. But if one uses the phrase strictly, it is equally obvious that it is all nonsense. *Here* is your so-called lottery paradox, paraphrasing Nelkin's earlier presentation:

The "Justification" Paradox

1*. Jim could justifiably believe that his ticket t_1 will *probably* lose.

2*. If Jim could justifiably believe that his ticket t_1 will *probably* lose, then he could justifiably believe that t_2 will *probably* lose, he could justifiably believe that t_3 will *probably* lose . . . and he could justifiably believe that $t_{1,000,000}$ will *probably* lose.

So,

3*. Jim could justifiably believe that *probably* t_1 will lose . . . and Jim could justifiably believe that *probably* $t_{1,000,000}$ will lose. (1*, 2*) . . .

Well, let's not go any further. It is clear that "justified belief" is not closed under conjunction, and that is the solution to the paradox—which *strictly speaking* is not the lottery paradox that we discussed earlier even though *loosely speaking*, it might be expressed in exactly the same terms. If one has a justified belief that probably p and a justified belief that probably q, then it does not follow that one has a justified belief that probably p & q. One *does* have a justified belief that probably p and probably q since it is not justification that is not closed under conjunction—it is *probability*. It does not follow from the fact that each ticket will probably lose that all the tickets will probably lose—of course! However, there is a giant conjunctive proposition that *is* entailed by the set of propositions that t_i will probably not win, i taking values from 1 to 1,000,000. That giant proposition is that t_1 will probably not win & t_2 will probably not win & ... & $t_{1,000,000}$ will probably not win. One is justified in believing that giant conjunctive proposition, just as, when rolling a die, one is justified in believing the conjunctive proposition that one will probably not roll a 1 or a 2 and one will probably not roll a 3 or a 4, each of whose conjuncts one justifiably believes, although one is not justified in believing that one will probably not roll a 1, 2, 3 or a 4. That it is probability and not justification that is not closed under conjunction is completely obscured if one uses 'justified belief that p' indiscriminately to refer to justified belief that p and mere justified belief that probably p. Neither does one's solution help solve the two other versions of the lottery paradox discussed in section 2.1.2 in which the phrase 'justified belief' is used strictly. Nelkin's unwillingness to countenance denying the conjunction rule for justified belief is entirely vindicated.

Back to the preface. A meticulous author might very well be justified in believing that each statement in his book is probably true, and yet not be justified in believing that probably all the statements in the book are true—indeed, he might very well be justified in believing that probably not-$(p_1$ & p_2 & ... & $p_n)$, or even the stronger categorical counterpart of that proposition. If one uses 'justified belief that p' indiscriminately to refer to justified belief that p and mere justified belief that probably p, again, the *obvious* solution to *this version* of the paradox of the preface is that "justified belief" is not closed under conjunction. But it is not because justification is not closed under conjunction, it is because probability is not closed under conjunction. Our author is most certainly justified in believing probably p_1 and probably p_2 and ... and probably p_n; he is not justified in believing probably $(p_1$ & p_2 & ... & $p_n)$.

What, then, of a version of the paradox of the preface that does not trade on a loose usage of 'justified belief'? We suppose that there is a meticulous author who is *really* justified in believing each and every one of the statements that he makes, and yet is really justified in believing that at least one of them is false. I am not sure that we have the materials for a genuine paradox—it is too easy to determine what we should say, on my view of justification and many others. The hypothetical situation is impossible. Such a meticulous author is not justified in believing each and every statement in his book. One of them expresses an unjustified belief— he just does not know which one. Transposing the "solution" according to my view of justification: there is some proposition p such that the author says that p and yet he does not know that p, but he does not know which statement(s) place him in that situation, and so can do nothing about it—at least without further inquiry. Further, it is perhaps questionable that many modest but *meticulous* authors would really have a justified belief that some statement they have made is false, strictly speaking. Rather, they will have justified beliefs that at least one of their statements is *probably* false.

Of course, if we are not speaking strictly, and in nonphilosophical contexts it is pedantic to do otherwise, it is perfectly appropriate to say that such authors justifiably believe that at least one of the statements in their book is false. I might well so speak in discussing this book with nonphilosophers. The preface to this book is addressed to philosophers, however, and it presents no genuine paradox.

2.5   More on Defining Knowledge

Our definition of justification, unlike its rivals in the vast literature on the matter, is extremely simple: a belief that p is justified if and only if its possessor knows that p. This is a pleasing sign. Speaking fully generally, a complex account of some matter is, I suppose, more likely to be true than a simple account. But a simple account is more likely to be true than any *given* complex account simply because there are more possible complex accounts than simple accounts. Moreover, the greater the complexity of the correct account of some matter, the harder it will be to discover (or even to formulate and comprehend) partially because of the prevalence of its equally complex rivals, and the less likely it will be that one will recognize that one has discovered it if one is lucky enough to hit upon it—it will be harder to discriminate from its equally complex rivals. (I do not intend to make these claims about any possible rational being; they are grounded in contingent facts about the limited minds of human beings.) It is hard to imagine any but the most hubristic philosopher coming up with a definition of justification containing multiple clauses and a couple of technical terms previously defined in terms of possible worlds or similarity metrics or whatever crying "Eureka! This is it! *This is justification!*" One would not be justified in believing any such definition of justification either by my definition or, I suggest, by any number of less stringent (for example, reliabilist) alternatives.

The subject of this section is my answer to, or evasion of answering, the question that my definition of justification inevitably provokes: what, then, is knowledge? To perhaps an even greater extent than with justification, the epistemological literature contains a host of complicated, multi-claused definitions that are, furthermore, dripping with technical or quasi-technical terms that are far less intuitive than the notion of knowledge itself. Quite apart from inviting the charge of attempting to explain the obscure by the more obscure, none of these definitions have met with widespread acceptance, and those that have excited sufficient attention have faced numerous counterexamples. Williamson (2000, 4) cites precisely the number of such failed definitions as a reason for concluding that knowledge should be considered a primitive. He considers the concept of knowledge to be indefinable. He holds that it should be taken as the basis for epistemological theory rather than the subject of definition.

That is also the position of this book, although what I say depends only on the identification of knowledge and justification, and not at all on its alleged indefinability. Knowledge cannot, of course, be defined in terms of justification, but numerous other definitions are quite compatible with most of what I have to say. Nevertheless, I wish to devote this section to arguing that a position like Williamson's is quite plausible. There is, *perhaps,* a sense in which knowledge can be defined in a complicated *functionalist* fashion, but that definition is much too complicated to be formulated and grasped by human minds. Even if we did *per impossibile* manage to formulate and grasp it, we would be unable to recognize that we had found the correct definition (drawing useful consequences is also likely to be beyond us). The metaphysics of functionalism is quite familiar (although its application to knowledge is novel); I shall outline it and apply it to the case of knowledge shortly. First, I will engage in some methodological preliminaries that make functionalism about knowledge (and other phenomena of philosophical centrality) attractive.

2.5.1 Concepts and Common Sense

There is a strong tradition within philosophy of respect for common sense. If a philosophical view has a consequence that is at odds with pretheoretical, intuitive, or *lay* opinion, then many philosophers, past and present, have taken that to be an almost decisive refutation of the view. This methodological stance is not universal, of course, and it is very easy to delude oneself into taking a profoundly counterintuitive view to be an expression of common sense. One of the most notorious examples is Berkeley's contention that material objects existing independently of the mind are a grotesque invention of sophisticated philosophers; the view of ordinary folks is that physical objects are nothing but a collection of ideas.

The traditional respect for common sense is a respect for commonsense *beliefs*. I wish to promote a respect for commonsense *concepts*—a respect that is much rarer than respect for commonsense beliefs, both historically and among contemporary philosophers.

A commonsense belief in the relevant sense is one that is almost universally held among ordinary people and to which all philosophers with a respect for common sense will also adhere. Of course, people ordinary and extraordinary flagrantly fail to use their common sense all the time in a perfectly reasonable sense of 'common sense', and this leads them to form absurd beliefs, but that is not the sense of 'common sense' that has concerned philosophers who respect common sense. For such philosophers, common sense is not an *ability* (only sporadically exercised by some) to form beliefs of a sort that are common because obvious. It is a collection of beliefs themselves that have almost universal appeal.

A commonsense concept, similarly, is one that is in universal or almost universal use among ordinary people. Many concepts of philosophical interest are commonsense concepts; the concept of belief is one, the concept of knowledge another (in the previous chapter I suggested that the concept of justification as something distinct from knowledge is not such a concept). Philosophers have been very interested in numerous commonsense concepts, but they have not had the kind of respect for them that they have had for commonsense beliefs, I claim. How so? What does respecting a commonsense concept, such as the concept of knowledge, entail?

Respect for a particular commonsense belief involves preserving it in relevant philosophical theories. One's theories *build* on that belief, one makes sure that it does not conflict with them and, ideally, is a consequence of such theories. One does not discard commonsense beliefs. Respecting commonsense concepts involves a preservation of those concepts. One does not replace those concepts with other, (allegedly) philosophically sophisticated concepts. One neither tries to define them in quasi-technical terms that are inevitably more obscure than the definienda, nor does one try to define commonsense concepts *away* in a similar fashion. One does not replace the notion of belief with quasi-technical concepts of *acceptance* or *degrees* of belief, as philosophers of science sometimes do. One does not replace the notion of personal identity with the quasi-technical concept of personal *survival* (Parfit 1986).

And one does not replace the notion of knowledge with quasi-technical concepts of justification, as some epistemologists have urged (Wright 1991). The commonsense concepts have been indispensable to people—*all* people—for a very long time (indeed, many of them are likely to be innate). It is hubristic to suppose that philosophical innovation might render them obsolete in the space of an article or two, or provide the means to replace them in principle with definitions. One should always be more confident in the *theoretical* utility of a pretheoretical concept than its proposed theoretical replacement or refinement; the history of philosophical analysis suggests that commonsense concepts conceal subtleties that even the most sophisticated definitions have failed to capture. Respect for commonsense concepts urges us to rest content with the concepts that God gave us.[43]

Of course, none of this is to deny that plenty of interest can be said *about* knowledge (and similar commonsense concepts), but just that what is said will itself ineliminably *employ* the concept of knowledge, and not in a merely preparatory fashion prior to a definition or elimination of knowledge. Commonsense respect for concepts does not demand an end to epistemology, just an end to epistemological analysis of concepts that are in perfect working order as they are.

It might be said that respect for commonsense concepts ignores the *metaphysical* aims of philosophical analysis. We cannot take the concept of knowledge to be in perfect working order until we have some account of how there could be any such thing as knowledge in the kind of world—a largely or entirely physical world—in which we find ourselves. "Natural-istic" analyses of knowledge, such as reliabilist definitions, serve precisely such metaphysical aims. We need no analyses to see how knowledge can be a part of the world as it is, however, as we will now see.

2.5.2   The Metaphysics of Common Sense: Functionalism

Functionalism is a view that has been propounded by philosophers of mind to explain how mental phenomena could be part of an entirely physical world. It comes in scientific and commonsense varieties; our concern will be with its commonsense variant. Our commonsense beliefs about a mental phenomenon such as the state of belief itself, for instance, form an implicit "theory" of the phenomenon. Let us stick with belief to illustrate how this is supposed to work. The implicit theory states a large number of charac-teristics that beliefs have, in particular their potential causal connections to other mental states and processes (desires, for example), behavior, and environmental stimuli. The totality of such statements implicitly defines a "functional role" for belief; any state that has that role, that has the char-acteristics that those commonsense statements specify, is a belief. In fact, our commonsense theory of the mind is taken implicitly to define *all* the commonsense mental states together, so a large number of physical states of the world situated in the appropriate functional relations to each other are the collection of beliefs, desires, memories, emotions, and so on that form an individual mind.[44]

A key feature of functional states is that they can be *multiply realized* (and, indeed, are assumed to be so in actuality in many cases). Many distinct phys-ical states can have the same functional role—for example, the functional role that is necessary and sufficient for a state to be a belief with a particu-lar content. If we think of the relevant physical states as *brain* states, states that have quite distinct neurophysiological characteristics might all possess the functional role necessary and sufficient for being beliefs that water is wet. It is perhaps overly simple to regard many mental states as *realized* by brain states alone since it is essential to their being the states that they are that they have certain relations to external phenomena. For example, it is a popular view that the belief that water is wet requires that there have been some kind of causal relationship at some time between the believer and water (Putnam 1975). Since the state that realizes a functional state is supposed to be sufficient for that functional state to obtain (although not *necessary*—that is the whole point of *multiple* realizability), states external to the mind containing water itself and their relations to brain states will have to be incorporated into the realizing physical state. Since it is a *historical* relation to water that is required to believe that water is wet, the realizing state will be one that entails that events of certain kinds occurred in the past.

Most criticisms of functionalism about mental states have focused on *phenomenal* states—sensations, emotions, and perceptual experiences. It is often claimed that no functional definition can capture the "phenomenal character" of such states, what it is like for a thinker to be in them. Williamson has argued that *knowledge* is itself a mental state. However, there is a far more orthodox sense than Williamson's in which it is relatively uncontroversial that knowledge is a mental state. (Williamson takes it that knowledge as opposed to mere belief can be fundamental to some psychological explanations.) Knowledge is a kind of belief. Since belief is not a phenomenal state, there is the prospect of a functional definition of knowledge that does not face the most pressing problems that functional definitions face. Knowledge is implicitly defined by commonsense beliefs about its relations to commonsense mental states (such as belief and understanding), the environment, and behavior, and perhaps other not so psychological states besides.

To claim that knowledge might be functionally defined in such a way is not to assume that Williamson is right to claim that knowledge is a mental state in a more controversial sense than the one mentioned above since there is absolutely no reason to suppose that only mental states can be implicitly functionally defined by our network of commonsense beliefs about them. Indeed, even if one adopts the minority position that knowledge is *not* a kind of belief, a commonsense functionalist definition is apparently no less viable. Common sense certainly holds that there are a large number of relations between the state of knowledge and uncontroversially mental states, and that is more than enough to support an implicit functional definition. (Indeed, implicit functional definitions of states that have no particularly noteworthy relations to the mental are unproblematic provided that they have enough relations to states of *some* kind or other.)

The states that realize functional states need not be restricted to the neurophysiological, and not just in the often-noted sense that a robot or a ghost might have electromechanical or ectoplasmic states that have the right functional roles to be mental states. Perhaps some "high-level" mental states are realized by "low-level" mental states that in turn are realized by the neurophysiological (and the neurophysiological is in turn realized by the quantum mechanical, and so on). (This position is open to those who doubt that mental states are physical in any interesting sense.) Perhaps knowledge is itself realized by a belief or beliefs and various relations between them and other mental states and the kinds of relations to the believer's external environment that proponents of "broad content" have stressed—perhaps knowledge is a "higher-level" mental state than belief.

The reader might be becoming impatient with all the speculation by this point. Exactly what might the functional definition of knowledge be that is supposed to be implicit in commonsense thought and talk about knowledge? And how might it be realized by a bunch of beliefs and other bric-a-brac? I have absolutely no idea, and I would not expect myself or anyone else ever to have any idea no matter how much time we devoted to the project of functionally defining knowledge. On the other hand, the project of functionally defining belief and every other mental state is in exactly the same primitive state. No one has ever come close to giving an adequate functional definition of belief, and few have really put in a serious attempt.[45] Nevertheless, the handwaving is, I contend, entirely respectable.

Functionalism can be advanced as a positive or a negative thesis. As a positive thesis, one proposes to discover just what belief (or knowledge) *really is*. Positive functionalism is a grand departure from respect for commonsense concepts. Functionalism as a negative thesis, on the other hand, hopes to do just enough handwaving to make the case that some philosophical problem is soluble in principle if we just put the time in (optimistic negative functionalism) or if we were a lot smarter than we in fact are (pessimistic negative functionalism). (Recall the remarks at the beginning of the chapter on complex definitions. Sufficiently complex definitions are superhumanly difficult to formulate, and superhumanly difficult to recognize even if dropped in one's lap.) Functionalism was originally proposed to do just enough handwaving to convince the philosophical community that, well, finding a place for the mental in an entirely physical world is perhaps not such a big deal after all. Functional definitions of mental states are available in principle, at least to the sufficiently diligent or superhumanly intelligent, and, even though we have not and never will formulate such definitions, there is no particular reason to think that some entirely physical states might not have the right functional roles to realize mental states. (Antifunctionalist friends of the phenomenal contest the latter claim, of course.)

(*Scientific* functionalists take it that we would not first have to codify commonsense principles concerning, say, belief before engaging in the grunt work of making implicit definitions explicit, which grunt work is detailed in Lewis 1970 among other places. That codification is humanly impossible, suspects the respecter of commonsense concepts. We could not come close to exhaustively codifying such commonsense principles, and if we were lucky enough to do so, we could not recognize that we had done so. The respecter of commonsense concepts is at most a pessimistic negative *commonsense* functionalist. The scientific functionalist takes it that psychological science would already contain a codified theory of belief and beliefs whose manipulation to produce Lewis-style definitions would be a merely mechanical matter. Of course, psychologists have not yet provided us with any such thing, making scientific functionalism as much of an exercise in handwaving as its commonsense variant, and an optimistic one at that.)

I am handwaving in this section not primarily to make a superficial case that knowledge is a physical state. I take it that *if* belief is physical enough for functionalist or other reasons for us to stop worrying about its place in a physical universe or about whether the universe really is merely physical, knowledge does not present any further problem. My handwaving is intended partially to make the case that we don't need to define knowledge at all—any more than we need to define belief. Any metaphysical worries about knowledge are soluble by the in-principle availability of a functionalist definition of knowledge, even if we will never have the definition and would not know it even if we did. The other purpose to my handwaving will occupy the next section.

2.5.3 The Diversity of Knowledge

Different theories of knowledge take their inspiration from different kinds of examples of knowledge. To many philosophers, one could not have a clearer case of knowledge than the visual beliefs that one forms quite unreflectively when one's eyes are in perfect shape and when one is observing ordinary-sized objects with ordinary properties in ordinary circumstances. Such instances of knowledge inspire accounts of knowledge that emphasize the reliability of the processes by which we form beliefs that constitute knowledge (Goldman 1992; Sosa 1991a) or the proper functioning of the faculties involved (Plantinga 1993a). These examples of knowledge are what Sosa has termed 'animal knowledge' (there is no great implausibility in suggesting that many animals have such knowledge).

The status of a belief as knowledge often relies on the quality of the evidence possessed by the believer and the degree to which he is diligent in drawing consequences from that evidence.[46] Such inferential examples of knowledge inspire a more evidentialist account of knowledge (and, of course, for many authors, of justification), combining both externalist and internalist elements (Alston 1986; Sosa 1991a). Knowledge of a more abstract or theoretical nature seems crucially to involve *understanding* (Zagzebski 1996). One only *knows* the knotty truths of physical or mathematical theories, some will suggest, when one understands how the whole theory works and what its important consequences are. Others will emphasize that it is one's *own* beliefs that must fit together or *cohere* if those beliefs are to constitute knowledge (Bonjour 1985). But, it will surely be said, we must also make room for the intuitive knowledge of those who form beliefs spontaneously without conscious evidential support because of extensive prior experience in some area, bringing us back to a more reliabilist view. It can seem that *conviction* or *confidence* is essential to knowledge, provided that one does not embrace unconscious or tacit knowledge to which the notion of conviction does not clearly apply.

It is exceptionally hard to give a definition of knowledge that all of these putative instances satisfy. It is far more tempting for an epistemologist to base his definition of knowledge around some of the examples and argue that others are not really knowledge at all. This is unfortunate since it seems rather intuitive—even a *fundamental constraint* on an account of knowledge—that what it takes to know such-and-such a proposition does vary quite a lot depending upon the kind of proposition in question and the kind of circumstances that a thinker is in.

Perhaps it is not impossible to give an all-encompassing definition consisting of some unconditional universal clauses that give characteristics that all instances of knowledge possess and some conditional clauses that say that *if* a proposition concerns subject matter *x* and a believer is in circumstances

y, then his belief constitutes knowledge just in case z. On the other hand, *if* a proposition concerns subject matter x' and a believer is in circumstances y', then his belief constitutes knowledge just in case z'. And so on. The hope would be that such a definition would not be so complex as to resist formulation, be unrecognizable if formulated, or draw useful consequences from.

Handwaving functionalism, however, enables us to accept the apparent diversity of knowledge at face value; such a definition is possible at most only *in principle,* and human intellectual limitations likely prevent its formulation. Our commonsense beliefs concerning knowledge implicitly define knowledge in an ungraspably complex fashion, which definition is satisfied by all the putative instances of knowledge . . . somehow (we are not going to worry about just how because we will not succeed in explaining it anyway). It is more likely that knowledge really is as diverse as it looks than that any unifying definition that has to jettison the diversity is correct (so respect for commonsense concepts urges). When we discuss testimony in chapter 3, we will see that the diversity of knowledge has important epistemological consequences. More generally, I will be from time to time rather promiscuous in my partial reliance on competing definitions of knowledge.[47] My working assumption is that reliabilists are right about what is a very important factor in making *some* cases of knowledge what it is, coherentism is a more accurate portrait of *other* instances of knowledge, foundationalists are more or less on the ball with respect to yet other cases, and so on—and we should not be remotely disturbed if we find instances of knowledge that do not fit very well with any approach.

2.5.4   Does the Contextualist Know When to Stop?

Are there any contemporary accounts of knowledge that I want absolutely no part of? There are—contextualist accounts of knowledge (DeRose 1995; Lewis 1996, for example). I will close this chapter by arguing for *invariantism* about knowledge.

A contextualist claims that knowledge *ascriptions* vary in their truth-conditions depending on the context in which they are uttered. The very same sentence ascribing knowledge of the very same proposition to the very same thinker might be true when uttered on one occasion and false on another even though the thinker himself has not changed in any relevant way between the two occasions.[48]

We make knowledge ascriptions not just to evaluate the beliefs of others, but to regulate our own actions. How we behave often depends upon whether we take ourselves to know some proposition or propositions. I will be focusing on one activity, inquiry, whose conduct is regulated by our self-ascriptions of knowledge (or a lack thereof). Knowledge is the *goal* of much inquiry. I will argue that contextualism about knowledge ascriptions is untenable in light of this fact.

'Inquiry' seems like a general enough term to cover almost any epistemic project. And one who is engaged in inquiry is often engaged in a *specific* inquiry centered around a specific proposition—he is inquiring into whether or not p, for some p. It seems truistic to say that he wants to know whether or not p. This truism reflects an important fact about specific inquiries: they often come to a proper end when the inquirer comes to know that p or comes to know that *not-p*.[49] He should cease his inquiry at that point for it has reached its goal.

Some will no doubt feel that the proper conduct of inquiry that is aimed at knowledge is to be understood more subjectively. The inquirer should cease his inquiry when he *believes* that he knows p (or, perhaps, *justifiably* believes that he knows p). Surely, however, if the inquiry is still important to its conductor, he will resume it if he comes to suspect that he did not know p after all—he will regard the inquiry as having terminated improperly. (Of course, the inquirer might be blameless in this matter insofar as he could not have been expected to behave any differently.) It is knowledge that is the goal of much inquiry, not belief that one knows—achievement of that goal is, however, mediated by an inquirer's belief that he does or does not know.

Inquiry is or involves action—sometimes exclusively mental acts of deliberation and so on, but often extramental actions, too. When an inquiry is over, an actor (or actors) stops performing an action (or actions), and when an inquiry is *properly* over, when it reaches its goal, an actor stops performing an action when he should. Actors want to reach their goals and cease the activities that led them to success. An actor engaged in an inquiry aimed at knowledge of whether p, for some p, wants to acquire that knowledge and stop the inquiry. Consequently, he will ask himself whether he knows that p or knows that *not-p*. If he thinks that he does, he will stop. If not, he will continue. If he *correctly* takes himself to know whether or not p, he will stop at the proper point, something that he will want to do.

In asking himself whether he knows that p, the inquirer is asking himself a question the truth-value of whose answer—'I know that p', 'I know that not-p', 'I do not know that p', or 'I do not know that not-p'—depends on the context in which it is uttered or thought, according to the contextualist. (Although knowledge ascriptions are propositional attitude ascriptions, and, on many views, all attitude ascriptions have context-sensitive truth-conditions, it is peculiar to epistemological contextualism that *self*-ascriptions show such variation.) The epistemic standards that are associated with the verb 'to know' and that determine the truth-conditions of knowledge ascriptions vary in their stringency from one context to another. Contextualists differ in their account of just what kinds of thing epistemic standards are and the manner in which they vary, and the details will be unimportant in what follows.[50]

How is an inquirer S whose goal is knowledge (that p, say) able to regulate his inquiry if contextualism is true? Let us suppose 'I know that p' is a sentence that, when uttered by S during his inquiry, is true in some contexts and false in others. S should stop his inquiry when he takes himself to know that p. The worry is that *sometimes* when he asks the regulative question, he will take himself to know that p and conclude that he should pack up his investigation. At other times (when there has been a context shift)—perhaps when he has already suspended the inquiry—he will judge that he does not know that p and so continue with the (perhaps temporarily terminated) inquiry. This is surely intolerable—continuing to act and ceasing to act are absolute matters. Whether one is or is not acting does not in any significant way depend on the context in which one uses the term 'acting'. In cases in which how one acts and whether one continues to act depend on judgments as to how one should act and whether one should continue to act, those judgments about what one should do must have invariant truth-values if they are properly to regulate action. And when those judgments about how one should act are directly tied to self-ascriptions of knowledge, those knowledge ascriptions must also have invariant truth-conditions, *pace* contextualism.

How might a contextualist argue that the worry is groundless? His best bet, I propose, is to argue that there are rarely, if ever, any inquirers in S's position. Rarely, if ever, will an inquirer's judgment that he does or does not know p shift its truth-value from one context to another, so rarely, if ever, will an inquirer be unable properly to regulate the end of his inquiry.

One strategy here might be to claim that a specific inquiry determines a single context. That is, a specific inquiry aimed at knowledge of whether or not p determines a single context for all questions about whether the inquirer knows whether p asked by the inquirer himself during the inquiry. This suggestion is untenable since once S comes to believe that he knows that p, he ends his inquiry. Further self-assessments of whether he knows that p, then, occur outside the context that was fixed by his original inquiry and are subject to contextual variation in truth-value. If S asks himself whether he knows p in some contexts, he will, by hypothesis, decide that he does not—at which point his previous inquiry would appear to have terminated improperly, and he will have to reopen his inquiry anew. S is still unable properly to regulate inquiry. (A further concern is that when inquiry into a specific proposition started for a particular inquirer is often extremely vague. That one is actively engaged in finding out whether or not some proposition holds is something that can gradually come to pass without any conscious determination that that is what one is going to do. That one of several possible epistemic standards governing an inquiry would be selected by such a gradual and perhaps initially fairly unreflective process is open to doubt.)

Another strategy is to claim that the use of knowledge ascriptions to regulate inquiry itself determines a single context. All contextual variation in the truth-values of knowledge ascriptions occurs when those ascriptions evaluate the epistemic pedigree of our beliefs or those of others in a way that is not directly tied to action. The regulative and evaluative functions of knowledge ascriptions are too closely related for this suggestion to be plausible. Many inquiries are collaborative. The question is not so much whether *I* know some proposition as whether *we* know some proposition. And for us to know whether or not p, we often need to find out whether or not various other propositions ('q' and 'r', say) hold first. Inquiry into these subordinate propositions is likely to be parceled out among us. So, for *me* to decide that we know that p, I might very well have to settle whether *you* know that q or whether *he* knows that r. If my ascriptions of knowledge to us are properly to regulate our inquiry, these evaluative ascriptions of others need to have an invariant truth-value as does the root regulative ascription.

A strategy of desperation is to claim that it is only in exceptional contexts, unconnected with action or its regulation, that the truth-conditions of knowledge ascriptions shift from those possessed in normal contexts. A discussion of skepticism would be the central example of such an exceptional context. It is extremely unlikely that a linguistic term has a degree of semantic freedom that only ever reveals itself in the obscurest backwaters of language use. Any claim to the contrary demands a strong argument. The point holds even if one claims that there are a few other relatively arcane contexts of language use in which the phenomenon occurs. (It is sometimes suggested that courtroom proceedings provide a context that shows the context-sensitivity of knowledge ascription truth-conditions. There are, of course, exceptionally high standards governing *something* in legal proceedings, but it is far from obvious that they govern the truth-conditions of knowledge ascriptions. In a trial, the cops can know that the accused is guilty. The judge can know it. The jury can know it. Everyone within and without the courtroom can know it. And yet a conviction cannot be secured since knowledge, however widespread, does not entail that legal standards of *proof* [contextually invariant in the relevant sense] can be met.) It is far more likely that we are disposed to make inaccurate knowledge ascriptions when we reflect upon skeptical possibilities.[51]

3   Testimony

3.1   Introduction

Two questions concerning testimony are the central subject of this chapter. The answers one gives to these questions, I will argue, should be intimately related, although the literature on testimony tends to focus on one or the other of the questions without exploring their relation. The first question is: under what conditions is a belief derived from the testimony of another *justified?* The second is: under what conditions does a belief derived from the testimony of another constitute *knowledge?*

Clearly, my answer to the first of these questions must be that a belief derived from testimony is justified if and only if it constitutes knowledge, since *any* belief is justified if and only if it constitutes knowledge on my view.[1] This answer leaves open a number of responses to the second question, however. In particular, I could consistently claim any of the following: (1) One knows that p on the basis of testimony just in case one believes that p on the basis of testimony that p given by one who knows that p. (2) One knows that p on the basis of testimony just in case one believes that p on the basis of testimony that p given by one who knows that p provided that one *believes* that the testifier knows that p. (3) One knows that p on the basis of testimony just in case one believes that p on the basis of testimony that p given by one who knows that p provided that one believes that the testifier knows that p *and* one has no reason to doubt that he knows that p.

I will not, however, be making any of these claims. Rather, I will argue that one knows that p on the basis of testimony just in case one believes that p on the basis of testimony that p given by one who knows that p provided that one *knows* that the testifier knows that p; I will call this view 'the KK view'.[2] I will argue against claims such as (1)–(3), which I will indiscriminately call 'the BK view' since the differences between them will not affect my arguments against the view. It will be useful to use the term 'U-justified' that we introduced in chapter 2 to cover both knowledge and the unknown unknown, (allegedly) justified beliefs and nothing else.[3] I will argue that the obvious strengthening of the BK view, the JBK view that requires one *(U-)justifiably* believe that the testifier knows that p requires further strengthening to the KK view if it is to be tenable *even if one does not (unlike me) identify justification and knowledge in general.* If one does not identify justification and knowledge, there is room for a weaker JBK answer to the *first* question; one is justified in believing that p on the basis of testimony that p provided that one is (U-)justified in believing that the testifier knows that p. Nothing weaker is tenable as an answer to the first question, however, I will argue.[4]

3.2   The BK View

3.2.1   Getting from an Answer to the First Question to an Answer to the Second

Tyler Burge (1993, 467) endorses the following "Acceptance Principle":

A person is entitled to accept as true something that is presented as true and that is intelligible to him, unless there are stronger reasons not to do so.

Translating the principle into terms that I have used in this work (and without significant loss, I think):

A person's belief that p derived from testimony that p is justified unless there are specific reasons not to accept the testimony.

Specific reasons to doubt someone's testimony are no doubt various in nature and cataloging them need not concern us. Certainly, if one knows, or justifiably believes, or merely suspects with or without justification that one's source is a pathological liar or has specific reasons to deceive oneself, or a group of which one is a member, or everyone, one is not justified in accepting the testimony of one's source without some substantial assessment of the reliability of the dubious testimony. But such situations are rare. In general, Burge is claiming that one's beliefs derived from testimony are justified *by default;* one has, in Elizabeth Fricker's terminology (Fricker 1987 and 1994), a "presumptive right" to accept testimony on Burge's view.[5] A belief derived from testimony can have its presumptive justification defeated, but the presence of defeaters is a departure from the norm; a particular act of testimony is innocent unless there are specific reasons to suspect its guilt. Hence Burge's use of the term 'stronger' in the Acceptance Principle. The answer to the question 'Stronger than what?' is 'Stronger than the strong reason one has to accept any testimony simply in virtue of its status as testimony'. Among other notable philosophers who have endorsed something along the lines of Burge's Acceptance Principle are C. A. J. Coady (1992) and the intellectual godfather of the default justification view, Thomas Reid (1970).

(A word on beliefs *derived* from testimony. I am using the term in a quasi-technical but quite natural fashion. One often believes things because of what someone says that are not in the appropriate sense derived from testimony, as many philosophers have noted. If someone says that he is hungry, one might form the belief that he speaks English because of his utterance. If someone says that he speaks English with a regional accent, one might form the belief that he speaks English with a regional accent [or even that he speaks English *without* a regional accent in the relevant sense] because of the way in which he said what he said rather than because of its content. One might even believe something on the basis of the content of someone's utterance without deriving it from the utterance in the relevant sense. Someone might say that he often utters non sequiturs *as* a non sequitur; one can believe what he said because of his saying precisely that without deriving that belief from his testimony in the relevant sense.

Deriving a belief from testimony in the relevant sense involves *something* like *trusting* what the testifier says. Deriving a belief from testimony does not really involve much like trust in a robust sense on my KK view. Some have claimed that trusting testimony is consistent with knowing that the testifier's "testimony . . . is correct" [Adler 1994, 266], whereas others have claimed that knowing that a testifier justifiably believes what he testifies to [and *a fortiori* knowing that the testifier knows what he testifies to] does not amount to trusting the *testifier* but trusting *oneself* [Graham 2000, 140]. There is something to be said for either position. Perhaps the best reconciliation of the conflicting claims is to say that, on any view according to which one has to have some positive justification for believing testimony such as the KK view, one trusts testimony when one justifiably accepts it in a similar sense of 'trust' to that in which one trusts one's senses when one forms beliefs derived therefrom.[6] In any case, I take it that the relevant notion of derived belief is clear enough.)

One who claims that beliefs derived from testimony are justified *by default* presumably intends to employ a notion of justification that also applies to beliefs that are not so derived. In particular, proponents of justification by default are claiming that testimonial beliefs (as I will henceforth call beliefs derived from testimony) are justified by default in the same sense that beliefs derived from, for example, perception are justified by default.

(It would be a mistake to claim that testimonial beliefs are justified by default in the sense that beliefs derived from *memory* are justified by default. Beliefs are not really *derived* from memory; they are *retrieved* from memory. Faulty retrieval—defective memory—might deprive such beliefs of justification that they had at the time of storage, of course. That is, one might cease to know what one formerly knew even though one has retained a belief that formerly constituted knowledge, and not because of new beliefs that one has formed since storage but because of what one has forgotten. Inaccurate recall of the content of the belief that one is trying to recall is one way in which this might occur. Accurate recall of a memory accompanied by inaccurate recall of evidentially related beliefs is perhaps another, although it is plausible that one need not retain *all*, or in many cases any, of the evidence that made a belief knowledge when it was first formed in order to retain that knowledge, even if what one does retain would not be enough to make the belief knowledge if it were formed *now*. Positively *inaccurate* recall of evidentially related beliefs, as opposed to mere failure accurately to recall such beliefs, is a different story.)[7]

In what sense are perceptual beliefs justified by default? Are the justified testimonial beliefs that do not constitute knowledge members of the unknown unknown class of justified beliefs or the known unknown class of justified beliefs on the default justification view? Justified *perceptual* beliefs that do not constitute knowledge are of the unknown unknown class.[8] I am justified in trusting my senses in general because, in general, when I form a belief that there is a barn over there on the basis of perception I *know* that there is a barn over there. "Bad luck" might land me merely with would-be knowledge, a belief that is justified in the unknown unknown sense, but I am not in a position to know that I do not know that there is a barn over there when I am in the land of fake barns, whether there is a barn over there or not (if I were in such a position, I would no longer have a justified belief that there is a barn over there). So, if the default justification that testimonial beliefs have is to be understood on the model of the default justification that perceptual beliefs have, testimonial beliefs justified by default constitute knowledge *unless* one suffers from "bad luck" in forming the testimonial belief.

Even if we set aside the perceptual analogy, justified testimonial beliefs that do not constitute knowledge must be members of the unknown unknown class. The only other options are that they are members of the known unknown class, or justified in some *sui generis* manner. I take the latter to be an unpalatable option. No one wants testimonial beliefs to be justified in some sense *proprietary* to testimony; the claim that testimonial beliefs are justified by default would lose all interest if that were so.

I will now argue at some length that a testimonial belief could not derive known unknown justified status by default if it is not knowledge.[9] That is, define a term 'K-justified' to correspond to 'U-justified'; a belief is K-justified if and only if it constitutes knowledge or is a member of the known unknown class of (allegedly) justified beliefs.[10] I will argue that a testimonial belief is not K-justified by default, although no confusion should result if I now drop the 'K' for the rest of the discussion. (I am not entirely sure that the position that testimonial beliefs are K-justified by default has any appeal at all, and dealing with all possible cases makes the argument somewhat intricate. If the position has no initial appeal to the reader, he will lose little by skimming the next couple of pages.)[11] A known unknown, justified belief that p is one such that the believer knows (or could know upon minimal reflection) that he does not know that p; what he does know is that *probably p* or something closely related thereto. Someone who had a known unknown, justified belief would either know that probably p independently of (in the typical case, prior to) hearing testimony that p or would derive that knowledge from testimony that p. If he knew that probably p independently of the testimony, the justification for his belief that p derived from that knowledge would also be independent of the testimony and irrelevant to our discussion.

So, we must consider the case of someone who hears testimony that p, but does not derive categorical knowledge that p from the testimony but merely knowledge that probably p and on that basis (allegedly) justified categorical belief that p. The problem that such a case poses is that, when conditions are right, testimony that p furnishes not just justified belief that

p but knowledge that p. If our case is a genuine possibility, we would have a three-tiered view of testimony that p. In the best case, the testifiee derives knowledge that p. In the intermediate case, he merely derives knowledge that probably p; this is the basis for a justified belief that p that does not amount to knowledge. In the worst case (when the testifiee is talking to a pathological liar, for example), he derives no knowledge and possibly (if he does not suspect the unreliability of his source) acquires an unjustified belief.

It is not possible for a testifiee to *derive* a belief from testimony with a superior epistemic status than the testifier himself has for his belief (at least if the belief's status as knowledge or as justified itself derives from the testimony).[12] If I derive knowledge that probably p on the basis of testimony, then the testifier *at least* knows that probably p (perhaps he knows that p). The form of the testimony from which I derive knowledge that probably p is either equivalent in all important respects to 'p' or to 'probably p'. If the latter, it is an instance of the *best* case, not the intermediate case. The testifier knows a fact (that *probably p*), states precisely that fact, and the testifiee comes to know that very same fact on the basis of his testimony. If the former, the testifier has either asserted that p when he does not know that p—he has made an unwarranted assertion, as we, following Williamson, explained in chapter 2—or he has done so when he does know that p.

Let us consider the unwarranted assertion first. One can come to know that p or probably p (or not-p or some entirely different fact) from unwarranted testimony that p by *inference* if one has appropriate background information. It is difficult, however, to see how one could *derive* knowledge *as opposed to acquiring justified belief* from an unwarranted assertion, even knowledge that is weaker than what the testifier testified to (that probably p as opposed to that p).

Let us, then, consider the warranted assertion. Clearly, if testimony has any epistemic worth whatsoever (and we will assume without discussion that it does), in some situations, a testifiee derives knowledge that p from the testimony that p given by someone who knows that p. In some situations, on the other hand, a testifiee fails to derive any knowledge from testimony that p given by one who knows that p, even if they believe that p on the basis of that testimony. The testimony of an innocent accused criminal that he is innocent (suppose that the testifiee was unacquainted with the accused prior to his testimony and that he offers no support for his claim whatsoever) does not enable the testifiee to know that the accused is innocent even if the testifiee should believe him.

It is unclear, however, how a testifiee could derive knowledge that *probably p* from testimony that *p* given by one who knew that *p*. The most natural suggestion is that the testifiee can derive such knowledge if he knows that *if* the testifier says that *p*, then he probably knows that *p*. Knowledge of such conditional facts is presumably quite common and will generally supply the testifiee with knowledge that probably *p* if he knows that the testifier said that *p*, and if, as seems plausible, knowledge that the testifier probably knows that *p* enables one to know that probably *p*. However, this knowledge that probably *p* is not *derived* from the testimony that *p*. It is obtained by inference from knowledge of what the testifier said and the conditional fact.

Nothing like "trusting" the testifier is involved. In whatever sense that testimony does involve trust, trusting testimony that *p* is not a matter of *first* believing (and knowing) that probably *p* and then inferring that *p*; it is a matter of believing that *p* at the outset. The known unknown, justified beliefs are not the kind of justified beliefs that testimony delivers by default when it fails to deliver knowledge. The intermediate case described above does not exist. If one hears testimony that *p*, one either derives knowledge that *p* therefrom, or, I suggest, one *derives* no knowledge at all.

One might nevertheless *obtain* a justified belief that *p* without obtaining knowledge that *p*; ultimately, of course, I deny that this is possible, but we will entertain the notion for the present. One's belief that *p* does not derive its justification from the testifier, for the only thing that the justifier has that he can *transfer* to the testifiee is the status of his belief that *p* as knowledge. If the testifier has a known unknown, justified belief that *p*, then he can unwarrantedly assert that *p*, in which case the testifiee cannot *derive* either knowledge that *p* or knowledge that probably *p*, although he might gain knowledge of either through inference if the circumstances are right. Or the testifier can with warrant assert that probably *p*, in which case the testifiee can derive knowledge that probably *p*. In neither case is justification *as opposed to* knowledge transferred.[13]

We have now finished the argument that testimonial beliefs are not K-justified by default. (What if the testifier has a U-justified belief that *p*? Might that kind of justification be transferred to the testifiee? Obviously, knowledge can be transferred to the testifiee since that is just to say that there is testimonial knowledge. So, we want to know if U-justification that falls short of knowledge, that possessed by the unknown unknown beliefs, can be transferred to the testifiee. We are still, of course, searching for the kind of justification that a testimonial belief is supposed to have by default, and we shall return to the question of whether the testifier can *transfer* the U-justificatory status of unknown unknown, justified beliefs to the testifiee along with the beliefs themselves after we have explored the default justification question further.)

Are testimonial beliefs U-justified by default? An unknown unknown, justified belief is *would-be* knowledge. It does not amount to knowledge because of bad luck grounded in the believer's external environment. Had things gone better in that environment, the believer would have known what he merely justifiably believes. If the testifiee gains a U-justified belief that *p* by default from testimony that *p*, then he gains knowledge that *p* in favorable circumstances—and favorable circumstances are themselves the default, unfavorable circumstances that do not lead to knowledge being the exception rather than the rule. In unexceptional circumstances, one who acquires a belief that *p* from testimony that *p* knows that *p* if beliefs derived from testimony are U-justified by default. A Burgean answer to our first question—under what conditions are testimonial beliefs justified?—entails a BK answer to our second question—under what circumstances do testimonial beliefs constitute knowledge? If the BK view is untenable in answer to that second question, a Burgean answer to the first will also be untenable. An argument against the BK view is also an argument against the default justification view.

I will argue that the BK view is untenable, however one elaborates the view. One detail that I will assume is that one who derives knowledge that *p* from testimony that *p* believes that the testifier knows that *p at least implicitly.* One implicitly believes propositions that one has not explicitly entertained (but understands) if one would explicitly believe them reflexively if one were to entertain them. For example, one implicitly believes that New York is less than a million miles from London.[14] It would not involve any nontrivial cogitation to form an explicit belief in that proposition upon considering it. (These sketchy remarks are not intended to constitute a *definition* of implicit belief: counterfactual definitions of implicit belief face the kinds of problem that are endemic to counterfactual definitions in general. One example commonly given in the literature is the proposition that one is speaking too loudly. One might in some sense be disposed to believe that proposition reflexively upon explicitly entertaining it without in any sense believing it beforehand. I am aiming merely to characterize what I mean by 'implicit belief' since the notion is, I take it, fairly intuitive.)[15] Certainly, a testifee who was disposed explicitly to believe that the testifier did *not* know that p, upon entertaining the proposition that the testifier did not know that p sufficiently reflexively (and hence he already *implicitly* believes that the testifier does not know that p), would be irrational if he believed that p on the basis of testimony that p, and would not, in any case, know that p on that basis (which amounts to the same thing on my view, of course). Moreover, anything less than an implicit categorical belief that the testifier knows that p seems to prevent the testifee deriving knowledge that p from testimony that p. If the testifee implicitly believes that the testifier only *probably* knows that p, he derives at best knowledge that probably p from testimony that p (and such knowledge is arguably inferential rather than derived from testimony in the relevant sense). If the testifee has no implicit belief on whether the testifier knows that p or implicitly believes that he probably does *not* know that p, it is all the more plausible to say that he cannot derive knowledge that p from testimony that p.

Before mounting an argument against the BK view, let us return briefly to the question of whether *mere* justification can be transferred from testifier to testifee. Suppose that I am in the land of fake barns and have an unknown unknown, justified belief that there is a barn over there (true or false). I tell you that there is a barn over there, and you believe me. Is your belief U-justified? Well, in happier and unexceptional external circumstances, I would know that there was a barn over there. Would you know that there was a barn over there on the basis of my testimony in those circumstances? On the BK view, you would, and so, on the assumption that there is such a thing as unknown unknown, justified belief, it would seem that you have just such an unknown unknown, justified belief that there is a barn over there. U-justification has indeed been "transferred" through testimony. I will return to this matter later to consider how views that are more stringent than the BK view that nevertheless endorse unknown unknown justification should answer this question.

3.2.2 Against the BK View

We are all good at something. We are all better at something than some other people. Sometimes, we do not know that we are better at things than others even though we are. But in many cases, we do know that we are better at certain things than some other people. And in many cases, we can name some of those others who are worse at some things than we are. Sometimes, those others also know that we are better than them at those things. In other cases, those others do not know that we are better than them at things at which we are in fact better than them. They might even believe that they are better than us. I, along with many of my readers, am a philosopher, and I know that I am a better philosopher than many philosophers that I might name. There are many philosophers who are better philosophers than I am; in some cases, I know this, and they know this. In other cases, I do not know this although they do, and vice versa.

I might tell someone who has absolutely no philosophical expertise whatsoever that I am a better philosopher than someone than whom I know that I am a better philosopher. The individual to whom I testify is not just relatively clueless about philosophy itself, let us suppose, but he also has no idea which philosophers are better than others; he has absolutely no opinion, informed or otherwise, on these matters. I submit that he cannot know that I am a better philosopher than the poorer philosopher just because I told him that I was. He has no acquaintance with philosophy or philosophers, including myself and my poorer counterpart. I do know that I am a better philosopher than my poorer counterpart, but I cannot transmit knowledge of that fact to an uninformed bystander simply by asserting it. I might, of course, be able to make a compelling case that I am a better philosopher that would enable the bystander to know that I am better, but let us suppose that I make no such case even if I could: I simply assert that I am the better philosopher. The BK view cannot accommodate such a situation: if I know that I am the better philosopher, and the testifiee believes me when I state that I am (believing at least implicitly that I know that I am the better philosopher), in the absence of reasons to doubt what I say, he will know that I am the better philosopher.[16]

This is a simple argument against the BK view, and hence, given the discussion above, also an argument against the default justification view. There are many equally plausible candidates for knowledge that is much harder to transmit than the BK view seems to entail. It is a near truism that there is much knowledge that it is practically impossible to impart to those much younger than ourselves as almost anyone will admit, whether he is elderly, middle aged, a young adult, an adolescent, or an older child with respect to those in all the younger age groups. That near truism is likely to command assent from anyone old enough to understand it. There are many things that we might tell our juniors that they might even believe if we were to tell them—but they will not know. With age comes wisdom; *how much* wisdom it brings will, of course, vary from individual to individual, but it always brings some knowledge that one has to learn for oneself and that cannot easily be transmitted via testimony.[17] Indeed, many will agree that some knowledge simply cannot be transmitted by testimony: one just has to figure it out for oneself. I do not propose to argue for the latter claim, both because it is not central to the discussion and because, if you doubt it, I cannot convince you. You really need to learn it on your own. Even if you believe me, you will not know. Neither will I give examples of such untransmittable knowledge. Examples that some will find compelling will not be compelling to others (because of a difference in age or experience, for instance).

What might a defender of the BK view and the associated default justification view say in response to this argument? As already emphasized, I have not defined the BK view very precisely since my arguments against it are general enough to apply however one fills in the details. However, one detail that most adherents of the BK view will insist on is something corresponding to the "unless there are stronger reasons not to do so" clause in Burge's Acceptance Principle. I will use the phrase 'the stronger reasons clause' to denote whatever specific clause the defender of the BK view might choose. By default, one knows that p from testimony that p provided one believes that p, but the default can be overridden. If there are good reasons to doubt the particular testimony in question or any testimony from the testifier or some salient group to which he belongs, one cannot know that p just by accepting testimony that p, and neither is one justified in one's testimonial beliefs so formed. Let us consider someone who knows that he can run faster than anyone else who lives in our neighborhood. Perhaps he knows that to run even nearly as fast as he can requires sufficient training and competitive effort that he has noticed anyone in the neighborhood with such dedication at the gym or on the track; and he knows that he can run faster than any of those people because he has raced them time and again. Suppose that the runner tells a bystander with no knowledge of who does and who does not run in the neighborhood that he is the fastest runner in the vicinity. It might be suggested that the very nature of the claim raises the standards for testimonial knowledge and justification well beyond the default. One cannot know *that* kind of claim without some positive reasons for accepting it, and that is true of the entire class of suggested counterexamples to the BK view. For some claims, perhaps, the standard for acquiring knowledge is raised so far above the default that it is practically impossible to verify the testimony of another without in effect coming to know or have a justified belief in the claim testified to that constitutes knowledge or is justified independently of the testimony. Some things one just has to figure out for oneself.

I do not disagree with these suggestions. *Of course,* some propositions are harder and perhaps even impossible to know by testimony than others—that is just the point that I am making. What I disagree with is the claim that this fact is consistent with the BK view. It amounts, rather, to *abandoning* the BK view. Whole classes of testimony cannot transmit knowledge without extensive checking *because of their content* not because of exceptional features of particular instances of testimony such as the testifier's reputation as a liar.[18] The default justification and BK views lack any pretense that they had to being distinctive views (or any views at all) if any apparent counterexample can be swept under the rug of the stronger reasons clause. If we do not restrict the application of such a clause to defects in *particular* testimony (including defects in the particular testifier or *testifiee,* on which more below) that is exceptional in the added stringency required for justification and knowledge when compared with relevantly similar acts of testimony—similar, for example, in their particular content (our runner is the fastest runner in the neighborhood) and *kind* of content (claims concerning someone being better at some physical activity than others are)—the BK view is not a determinate view at all. If the BK and default justification views are to be determinate views, we need to be able to say that *this* piece of testimony demands higher standards, but *most* testimony like that in all relevant senses does not—all that is required for justification in most cases is belief, and all that is required for knowledge in most cases is the added fact that the testifier to p knows that p.

One important constraint on the status of testimonial beliefs as justified or unjustified will be how well they cohere with other beliefs that the testifiee already holds. Facts about particular testimony or particular testifiers are just one way in which the "stronger reasons" clause will come into force. The *content* of testimony can reasonably be taken to trigger the clause if it conflicts with what one already believes without depriving the default justification view of force—the particularity of the testimony here resides in the testifiee. Of course, one should often abandon some of one's previous beliefs rather than refuse to accept the testimony, but such a response to testimony will often require proper consideration of how to weigh the testimony on the one hand and one's prior beliefs on the other; acceptance of the testimony will not be justified *by default.* This does not increase the plausibility of the default justification position, however. Rather, it threatens to saddle a believer who lives up to allegedly appropriate epistemic standards with a bunch of junk beliefs from which he will have to extricate himself at a considerable cognitive strain.

Suppose that one has a relatively sparse set of beliefs on some topic. Since one is justified in believing what one is told on that topic by default, one will be justified in believing the first testimony on the topic that one encounters unless there are stronger reasons not to. Those stronger reasons are likely to be thin on the ground until one builds up one's stock of beliefs on the topic. And it would seem to be entirely rational to build up that stock of beliefs as quickly as possible. After all, if one were to believe what one is told, one would be justified in one's belief unless the stronger reasons clause applies, which by hypothesis is rare at this stage of one's inquiry. Once one has such a stock of beliefs, even if they are largely false, the stronger reasons clause kicks in when one encounters conflicting testimony. For sure, conflicting testimony often transforms one's previously justified beliefs into unjustified beliefs. Perhaps everything comes out in the wash and at the end of inquiry one is likely to have a stock of beliefs that are, by and large, justified. But stricter standards for when one is justified in accepting testimony will save the believer who lives up to those standards a lot of trouble.

This is a problem for the default justification view alone; one does not face the problem if one endorses the BK view without endorsing the associated default justification view. The entailment from the default justification view to the BK view is arguably unidirectional. Even if a proponent of the BK view conjoins it with a view on justification, he can say that a testimonial belief that *p* is justified just in case it is U-justified—just in case the testifiee would know that *p* in unexceptional circumstances, where he does not suffer from "bad luck." On some matters, perhaps most testimony one encounters does not express knowledge on the part of the testifiers. Believing testimony on such matters is not enough to give one U-justified beliefs. It is not bad luck in hearing testimony on such matters to encounter a testifier who does not know; it is good luck to encounter one who does. The BK view, without an unacceptably expansive reading of the stronger reasons clause, is still committed to saying that in cases of such good luck, one does know that p simply by believing testimony that p, but that is a separate concern about the BK view. A proponent of the view is not committed to the default justification of testimonial belief—or at least it requires further argument to show that he is. Since I have other arguments against the BK view itself, it will not do a proponent of the view much good to disavow the default justification view if those arguments are good, and I will not explore the matter any further.

To finish our discussion of the BK view, I will consider the transmission of testimonial knowledge. If I derive knowledge that p from testimony that p, then I in turn should be able to transmit that knowledge to others through testimony. Suppose that my belief that p does derive from a testifier who knew that p. As previously argued, I will believe implicitly that the testifier knew that p when he testified—at least provided that I remember that my belief came through testimony, and let us suppose that I do. (If I forget that fact, my forgetfulness will surely not render a belief knowledge that did not constitute knowledge when I did remember its origin.)

If I do not justifiably believe that the testifier knew that p, then it will be, I suggest, epistemically irresponsible for me to believe that p and doubly irresponsible to tell another without qualification that p. Doubly irresponsible because my belief that p is not justified, and neither will be the belief of another that is derived from mine through my irresponsible testimony. If I *did* know that p through testimony that p, despite having no justification for believing that the testifier knew, then one who in turn receives my testimony that p ought to be in a position also to know that p and will know that p if he believes and does not have "stronger reasons" to doubt my testimony than to believe it. Such a chain of transmitted testimony, which might be extended indefinitely, seems far too shaky to be a chain of transmitted *knowledge*. The BK view entails that it is just such a chain.

One response to this argument is for the proponent of the BK view to adopt a strengthened version of the default justification view in conjunction with the BK view itself. It is not just testimonial beliefs that are justified by default, but also the testifiee's associated beliefs that testifiers know what they testify to. Consequently, the conjoined view is not committed to the claim that a testifiee who does not justifiably believe that the testifier that p knows that p (although he does) nevertheless knows that p if he believes the testimony that p. This is, I suggest, an extremely unpromising response. The question arises once again: in what sense of 'justified' is a testifiee justified by default in believing that the testifier knows? He is not K-justified in believing that the testifier knows by default since that entails that the testifiee knows that the testifier that p probably knows that p by default. That is not a philosophical claim, it is an empirical one and a false claim at that. Is the testifiee U-justified in believing that the testifier knows by default? If so, in unexceptional circumstances, when he does not suffer from external bad luck, the testifiee *knows* that the testifier knows. The BK view conjoined with the strengthened default justification view entails a strengthened KK view! Knowledge that the testifier knows is apparently very easy to come by—it is the default. I have argued and will argue in more detail below that knowledge that the testifier knows is in *many* cases fairly easy to come by— but it is far from the default for testimony in general. The KK view is *prima facie* much more plausible than the strengthened default justification view by anyone's lights.

We also arrive at (my more moderate version of) the KK view if we adopt an extremely liberal view of when the stronger reasons clause of the default justification and BK views applies. Those views, if they amount to anything determinate, are arguably equivalent on such a reading of the clause to my KK view and its counterpart for justified testimonial belief (if one believes that there is a distinction, of course). Let us consider a case where it really *is* easy to acquire testimonial knowledge and *a fortiori* justified testimonial belief. You ask me what time it is, and I, knowing what time it is, tell you. *Ceteris paribus,* you now know what time it is. Such easy testimonial knowledge does not, however, support the claim that at least some of one's testimonial beliefs are justified and constitute knowledge by default in the sense in which proponents of the BK and default justification views intend. For it is quite plausible that in this kind of case you know, not just what time it is, but you also know that *I* know what time it is. Ultimately, I will be arguing that that is why *you* also know what time it is, but the claim about what you know that I know is plausible quite apart from those arguments. I suggest that all intuitive cases of easy testimonial knowledge turn out similarly: they are also intuitively cases where it is easy to know that the testifier knows what he testifies to. I suggest also that a continuum of cases in which it is progressively harder to acquire testimonial knowledge will also be a continuum of cases in which it is progressively harder for the testifiee to know that the testifier knows and that a very expansive reading of the stronger reasons clause of the BK view will simply track that fact.

A continuum of cases in which it is progressively harder to acquire justified testimonial belief that does not amount to knowledge will also be a continuum of cases in which it is progressively harder justifiably to believe that the testifier knows that to which he testifies. The counterpart of the KK view for justified testimonial belief if one wants to traffic in such things is: one is justified in believing testimony that p if and only if one is U-justified in believing that the testifier knows that p.[19] If I in fact do not know what the time is, but merely have a U-justified belief about the time, true or false, perhaps because I have a stopped watch (which might be of Russell's variety that in fact happens to show the correct time when you ask me the time), you can acquire a U-justified belief as to the time from my testimony on the basis of a U-justified belief that I do know the time—you would have known both the time *and* that I knew the time in more favorable external circumstances.

Having abandoned the BK view, there is one more avenue someone might try before accepting the KK view. The JBK view states that in order to know that p from testimony that p supplied by one who knows that p, it is necessary and sufficient to have a U-justified belief that the testifier knows that p.[20] The counterpart view on when one is justified in believing that p on the basis of testimony that p (that is, irrespective of whether the testifier knows that p or is even justified in believing that p or of whether p is even true) is identical in form to the JBK view itself: one has to justifiably believe that the testifier knows that p. That justified belief constitutes knowledge if and only if the testifier himself does know that p. This position on justification, as stated above, is also the position that a defender of the KK view should take *if* he distinguishes justification and knowledge (as this defender of the KK view, of course, does not). Hence, the argument that follows is an argument against the JBK view alone and not against the associated position on justified testimonial belief. (The stopped-clock case shows that there is a sense in which *mere* justification can be transferred from testifier to testifiee on the conception of justified testimonial belief associated with the JBK and KK views.)

Of course, in my view, justified belief being knowledge, the *real* JBK view just is the KK view. But the KK view can be established as superior to the

JBK view even on the assumption that there are justified beliefs that do not constitute knowledge.

3.3   Against the JBK View

The JBK view certainly has notable advantages over the BK view. It can easily handle the fact that some knowledge is harder to transmit than other knowledge. Depending upon both the content of the testimony and the testifier (as an individual or as a testifier of a relevant kind), it is more or less difficult to have a justified belief that the testifier knows. If you ask someone the time, it is relatively easy to have a justified belief that the testifier knows the time; if a testifier asserts that he is better than another in his expertise in some field that you are not remotely familiar with, it is much harder to come to a justified belief that the testifier knows that he is better. As with the BK view, the testimonial beliefs that constitute knowledge on the JBK view are a superset (albeit a smaller superset) of those that constitute knowledge on the KK view. Every testimonial belief that constitutes knowledge on the KK view will constitute knowledge on the other two views since if one knows that the testifier knows, one justifiably believes that he knows and *a fortiori* believes that he knows. What we need to consider are the testimonial beliefs that constitute knowledge on the JBK view but *not* on the KK view and see whether they really do amount to knowledge.

Those testimonial beliefs are ones where the testifiee has a *merely* justified belief that the testifier knows in the unknown unknown sense of 'justified'. They are cases in which the testifiee has would-be knowledge that the testifier knows; in happier, unexceptional circumstances, he would know that the testifier knew. Now, the testifier *does* know that p in the relevant cases; otherwise, a proponent of the JBK view will say that the testifiee at best derives a merely justified testimonial belief that p from the testimony that p. So the testifiee has a merely justified, true belief that the testifier knows that p. This is not just structurally similar to a Gettier case: it *is* a Gettier case. That is, such a testimonial belief does not constitute knowledge contrary to the JBK view. Let us see why.

I will use a case that was first described by Gilbert Harman (1973) in a somewhat different context. I know that a political figure has been assassinated. I tell you that he has been assassinated (perhaps by reporting it in an early edition of the newspaper, as in Harman's original story, perhaps just by informing you face to face), and I am in general a reliable source on such matters (as is my newspaper, if we run the story that way). That is, from me one normally gains knowledge on such matters. However, a huge coverup of the assassination has been launched. There are a large number of people disseminating the misinformation that the assassination was unsuccessful (perhaps by recalling the original edition of the newspaper and distributing a far greater number of copies of a later edition containing the misinformation, as in Harman's original story, perhaps just by spreading the misinformation face to face). You have not encountered any such people (the erroneous newspapers or the individuals themselves), however. All you have heard is what I have told you (in print or otherwise).

If you read my newspaper or talk to me in unexceptional circumstances, you know what I report and you *know* that I know what I report. In these exceptional circumstances, however, we cannot say that. You do not know that the political figure has been assassinated (Harman's original point), you merely have a justified belief that he has. You *also* have a merely justified belief that I know that the political figure has been assassinated, which, by hypothesis, I do. The JBK view is false, and for similar reasons to those that render the traditionally said-to-be-traditional JTB analysis of knowledge false. Just as a justified, true belief need not amount to knowledge, a justified, true belief that a testifier knows that p will not necessarily enable one to know that p even if one believes the testimony. The land of fake newspapers is the land of fake barns all over again.

The KK view provides a diagnosis of Dretske's "cognitive cul-de-sac" (Dretske 1982) as well as Harman's newspaper case. George regularly misidentifies Chianti as Bordeaux because of geographical ignorance; he thinks that Tuscany is in the Bordeaux region of France rather than a region in Italy. However, George accurately identifies both Medoc, which is actually a Bordeaux and known to be so by George, and Chianti—he simply inaccurately classifies the latter wine as a Bordeaux. Suppose that George in fact drinks a Medoc on one occasion. George knows both that he drank a Medoc and that he drank a Bordeaux. He tells Michael that he drank a Bordeaux (and does not specify that it was a Medoc); Michael knows that George can accurately identify Chianti as Chianti and Medoc as Medoc. Michael does not know that George drank a Bordeaux even if he believes what George said and even though George knows that he did drink a Bordeaux. Michael is beyond the cul-de-sac; the road terminates with George.

Whether or not Michael is aware of George's propensity to misclassify some wines as Bordeaux, the fact that George does so is a *defeater* for Michael knowing that George drank a Bordeaux. Why is this so? Because it is in the first instance a defeater for Michael's knowing that George knows that he drank a Bordeaux. Given George's propensity to misclassify some wines as Bordeaux, Michael cannot know that George's testimony that he drank a Bordeaux expresses knowledge on George's part—for all Michael knows, George drank a Chianti. Even though Michael might be unaware of George's tendency to misclassify Chianti, he would need to know that tendency had not been manifested in this case to know that George knows that he drank a Bordeaux. Had George said that he drank a Medoc, Michael would have known that George drank a Medoc—in that case, Michael would have known that George knew that he drank a Medoc.

3.4   The KK View

The KK view clearly states conditions that are *sufficient* to know that p if one forms the belief that p upon hearing testimony that p (although there is some concern in the literature about whether one's knowledge is *derived* from the testimony, which I will address below).[21] If I know that you know that p, then I know that p is true, and I also understand the proposition that p, else I would not be able to know (and hence believe) that you know that p. So knowledge that p is true entails knowledge that p in the circumstances. What we need to consider are objections to the claim that the KK view states accurate necessary conditions for testimonial knowledge.

The KK view receives very little discussion in the literature on testimony, although Jonathan Adler has defended the view, in part, by rejecting the JBK view, for some of the reasons given in the previous section (Adler 1996). A brief exception is one paragraph in Graham 2000, in which Graham says that the position is "arguably too demanding." The idea in *particular* cases of testimony appears to be that if one knew that the testifier knew that p, then one would oneself know that p *independently* of testimony that p. In *general*, one might claim that so much of our knowledge derives from testimony that we could know very little if testimonial knowledge required knowing that the testifier knew—the requisite second-order knowledge (if I might call it that although it is knowledge about the knowledge of another rather than knowledge about one's own knowledge) is not, in general, possible without reliance upon previous testimony, and so a regress threatens.[22]

The general point will require a lengthy response; the point about particular testimony can be dealt with much more swiftly. It is common to know such things as that a certain individual *S* is an authority on the best Chinese restaurants in town. (Such knowledge itself depends heavily on testimonial knowledge, but we will address that when we turn to the general point.) In particular, one often knows such things as that if *S* says that *r* is a good restaurant, then it is. Why? Because *S* will know that *r* is a good restaurant if he says it is. That is, we know that if *S* says that *r* is a good restaurant, then *S* knows that *r* is a good restaurant. Suppose that *S* does say that *r* is a good restaurant to us; we now know that he said that *r* is a good restaurant, and we know that if he said that *r* is good, then he knows that *r* is good. A trivial inference gives us knowledge that *S* knows that *r* is a good restaurant. And so we know that *r* is a good restaurant since the KK view clearly states sufficient conditions for testimonial knowledge. Our knowledge in this particular case essentially depends on *S*'s testimony that *r* is a good restaurant; we would not know that if he had not said it.[23]

Our knowledge that the testifier knows often depends heavily upon the testimony itself in a quite different way. Often enough, one can tell that someone knows what they are talking about because of the way they talk—both from their manner (a certain characteristic confidence) and from the content of what they say.[24] Someone who says that *p*, where that *p* is (perhaps a part of) a very detailed account of some phenomenon, would not be capable of giving such an account unless he knew that *p*, and we know that. This is not to say that it is logically impossible to give such testimony and not know what one is talking about, of course! Just that it is not possible in a robust enough sense to interfere with knowing that one who gives such testimony knows what they are talking about.

Of course, the details of the particular case are very important. If it would be easy enough for one to be bamboozled by a charlatan testifying in some area of expertise, one will in many cases not know that the testifier knows even if he is in fact an expert and knows what he is talking about. In other cases, such a possibility is a mere possibility that will not interfere with one knowing that the testifier knows. Someone who, for example, had a propensity *apparently* to give a detailed listing of the most influential contemporary epistemologists and why they were so influential but who actually knew absolutely nothing about epistemology or epistemologists and fabricated his whole testimony does not exist, and even someone who knew no epistemology whatsoever can know that a given epistemologist knows that Alvin Plantinga is one of the big names in contemporary epistemology because of his testimony to that fact.

(Another condition clearly sufficient for one to know that p is one's knowing that *someone* knows that p. One can come to know that someone knows that p even if one does not know of anyone in particular who knows that p. For example, one might know that the individual who tells one that p is "parroting" the claim that p made by an unidentified source or sources who know that p—it is not necessary that the parrot himself know that p for oneself to know that p since that is not necessary for one to know that *someone* knows that p. Students are often in such a situation; they know that their teachers simply repeat claims made by unidentified knowledgeable sources. Jennifer Lackey [1999] describes an [arguably rather unorthodox] Catholic elementary schoolteacher who teaches Darwinism to her students although she does not believe, and hence does not know the truth of, the Darwinist claims that she makes.[25] That what the teacher says derives from the testimony of knowledgeable others is essential to the students gaining knowledge. If the teacher had come up with the theory of evolution by natural selection *on her own,* rejected it, and decided to teach it anyway, her students could not gain testimonial knowledge of the theory's claims from her. I hence do not regard Lackey as having presented a counterexample to the claim that, for a testifiee to gain testimonial knowledge that p, the testifier must know that p. There are testifiers who know the Darwinian claims behind the scenes in Lackey's example, and there have to be such for the students to come to know Darwinism from what the teacher says— and the students have to *know* that there are such, I contend, for reasons parallel to those given earlier in the chapter. The students might or might not believe that their teacher knows the Darwinist claims to be true; it is not any such belief that is the source of the students' knowledge of Darwinism, it is the students' knowledge that someone does know that those claims are true.)

Detailed consideration of just when one can know from the testifier's manner and the content of his testimony that he knows what he is talking about belongs more properly to the sociology of knowledge than episte-mology (if it belongs anywhere), so let us move on. Indeed, detailed consideration of just when one can know that the testifier knows depends so much on what is being said, who is saying it, and who is listening to it, that I imagine that little can be said that is sufficiently general to consti-tute philosophy and so to be of interest to philosophers qua philosophers; neither will a philosopher qua philosopher be competent to say much on the matter. What one can say is that just as knowledge in general is much harder to obtain in some cases than others depending on what is known and the circumstances of the knower, knowledge that another knows is no exception.

Very well, it might be said. If we take the large amount of knowledge that we already have for granted, perhaps it is not such a stretch to say that further testimonial knowledge requires us to know that the testifier knows, and that this requirement is easy enough to live up to in some cases, although much harder in others. But a very large part of the large amount of knowledge that we already have was derived from testimony. There is surely no prospect of a "global reduction" of testimonial knowledge to nontestimonial knowledge as Coady argues effectively at great length—consider as he does that our knowledge of what words mean is largely testimonial, and all other testimonial knowledge depends upon that.[26] We need testimonial knowledge from infancy onward if we are to know anything at all. And that means that something like the default justification view and/or the associated BK view is correct.

Elizabeth Fricker (1994) responds to this worry and to Coady in particular. Her view of testimony (Fricker 1994, 1987) is in some ways the closest position in the literature to my own since she demands that the testifee have some positive justification for believing testimony if testimonial beliefs are to be justified—testimonial beliefs are not justified by default. (Testimonial justification rather than testimonial knowledge is her concern, what we called "the first question" at the beginning of this chapter rather than the second. And, of course, justification is for her not identical to knowledge, functioning as something of a primitive concept for her as for so many epistemologists.) The term 'global reduction' is one that she uses, and she stresses that she is committed to no such position. She calls her denial that there is a "presumptive right" to testimonial belief a "local reduction" of the justification of *particular* testimonial beliefs that p to the justificatory status of beliefs in propositions other than p that the testifee already holds. Many of those other beliefs, she grants, might in turn depend on testimony for their justification.

A further similarity of her views to mine is that she stresses that the positive justification a testimonial belief requires need not involve any great effort on the part of the testifee. She says that having a *disposition* to withhold belief in p if there is anything fishy about the testimony and/or the testifier is in many cases enough to qualify as being justified in believing that *p*. Testimony that is not fishy does not require any process of assessment to be justifiably believed; simply believing it *if you would not have done so* were it fishy is enough. She also says that a testimonial belief can qualify as justified in virtue of how well it coheres with beliefs one already holds. Again, *something* is required for a testimonial belief to be justified—it is not justified by default—but it is a mistake to think that this requires that the testifiee perform some specific act of judging the worthiness of a piece of testimony. I agree with these points, adapting them to the case of testimonial knowledge (which for me, of course, is all that justified testimonial belief amounts to). Having the right dispositions can be a large part of knowing that a testifier knows, as can the coherence of testimony with one's prior knowledge.

The question of how one gets started with testimonial knowledge remains, however. Does a child lack testimonial knowledge entirely? (To Fricker herself, of course, one poses the question of whether children lack justified testimonial beliefs.) How then, does he ever get himself into a position (adulthood, for example) in which Fricker's local reductions can apply? Are children's testimonial beliefs justified by default even if adult beliefs are not? Does the BK rule hold for children's testimonial knowledge but not for adults'? How can that be?

Suitably elaborated in a number of possible ways, I think that it is reasonable to suppose that the epistemic standards for children's testimonial knowledge are lower than those for adult's in the sense that the relevant second-order knowledge is easier for them (which is still to apply a KK standard uniformly to children and adults)—I will sketch such elaborations below. But it is also reasonable to suppose that they are not lower and that children indeed lack testimonial knowledge (and hence justified testimonial belief). I will not endorse either possibility—since each possibility is a reasonable supposition, I cannot make up my mind (that is, form a justified belief) as to which holds, and the KK view is, I will argue, untroubled if either alternative holds.

The first answer to the question of how children get *started* with testimonial knowledge, and hence with knowledge in general, more or less, since so much of it beyond simple perceptual knowledge depends upon testimony is: they don't get started. The view that almost all knowledge depends on a base largely composed of testimonial knowledge that one acquires early in life is perhaps correct in a sense, but it should not be given a foundationalist reading. It is not the case that one acquires later knowledge only if one's

childhood beliefs *already* constitute knowledge. Rather, one's childhood beliefs are, at their genesis, unjustified; they do not constitute knowledge. The
child adds more and more unjustified beliefs and, as the (initially unjustified) picture of reality is filled in, it gets closer and closer to being a justified
picture of reality. A belief that was once unjustified becomes knowledge as
one acquires further beliefs—at least if one acquires the right beliefs, which,
by hypothesis, actual children in the actual world do. There is a lot to be
said for a *coherentist* view of knowledge (and I am not committing myself to
a coherentist *definition* of knowledge here, of course, partly, but not only, for
reasons stated in section 2.5) as opposed to a foundationalist view. Coheren-
tists propose just this picture of knowledge. What makes a belief knowledge
is how well it coheres with a sufficiently complete and coherent belief set,
and that plausibly is a big *factor* in what makes many beliefs knowledge.
The very same belief can fail to be a member of such a set at one time—in
the mind of a child—and become a member of such a set as more beliefs are
added and the child gets closer to adulthood.

None of this is to say that children are reprehensible in their testimonial
beliefs. We cannot blame them for forming beliefs as they do since, first, they
don't know any better, and, second, they cannot do anything else if they
want eventually to acquire knowledge. As stressed in section 1.3.4, we *teach*
children their *moral* obligations, we do not create them by our teaching, and
we do not blame them in many cases for their incessant violations. Perhaps
we should hold that children violate their *epistemic* obligations continu-
ously, and that they cannot do otherwise—indeed, in at least the epistemic
case, it is, in a very important sense, a very good thing that they violate
their obligations. If we are not foundationalists, exceptionless early flouting
of epistemic standards is compatible with (indeed, it is in practice essential
for) meeting those standards later in life. After all, it is incontestable that
children do not know a lot of what they believe (for example, because it is
false), and it should be equally incontestable that many of their beliefs are
unjustified by normal standards. They are neither unknown unknown, justified beliefs nor known unknown, justified beliefs; they would not constitute
knowledge of the proposition believed in unexceptional circumstances, nor
do the children know that the proposition believed is probable in their actual circumstances. The only relevant sense in which children's beliefs are
by and large "justified" is that they are blamelessly held, and if *that* is all
that one were to mean by claiming that children regularly form justified

beliefs, it would be a very uninteresting claim that can appear to be interesting only if one conflates blamelessness and some other epistemic value or values. Just *when* children make the transition from forming a large number of unjustified beliefs to forming far fewer unjustified beliefs is a matter of indifference to the epistemology of testimony.

On this view, children acquire little *testimonial* knowledge since their testimonial beliefs, although initially derived from testimony, come to constitute knowledge for coherentist reasons, not because they were derived from testimony. Indeed, when they come to constitute knowledge—and it is no doubt indeterminate when that occurs since knowledge is subject to vagueness, as is almost every other phenomenon—the testifiee will no doubt have forgotten the testimony from which his or her beliefs derive and in some cases will perhaps not even know that they derive from testimony at all. The testifiee will not ever perhaps come to know that the testifier in question knew the proposition to which he testified, which testimonial knowledge requires on the KK view. The coherentist process by which unjustified testimonial beliefs can come to constitute nontestimonial knowledge is not restricted to children. Adult testifiees can form unjustified testimonial beliefs that come to constitute knowledge in a coherentist manner; for that matter, as a result of testimony that p, an adult might form a belief that p that, at the moment of its formation, constitutes knowledge for coherentist reasons without the testifiee knowing that the testifier knows that p and that he would not have formed had he not heard the testimony. And this coherentist process might operate for children in tandem with the formation of testimonial knowledge if children are indeed capable of a significant amount of testimonial knowledge, a possibility that we will now discuss.

Can we do any better, then, for the poor kids? Can we make a case that they have a lot of justified testimonial beliefs (that is, testimonial knowledge) from the outset? Some have argued (e.g., Hawthorne [2004]) that certain cases in the literature that have been used to support contextualism about knowledge attributions—the view dismissed in section 2.5.4 that whether a knowledge attribution is true depends in part on the contextually varying standards that the ascriber employs for a belief to count as knowledge—in fact support a certain kind of "subject-dependence" (the term is Hawthorne's) in knowledge itself. Let us see how subject-dependence might help our children.

DeRose's Bank Cases (DeRose 1992) suggest that whether we are willing to say that someone knows that the bank will open on Saturday depends upon how important it is—to him or to us—that the bank is open. If he just wants ten dollars that he could obtain elsewhere it takes much less to know that the bank is open on Saturday than it does if he will go bankrupt and be evicted or shot by The Mob unless he can get money from the bank on Saturday. Stewart Cohen (1999) presents a similar case in which what it takes to be described as knowing when and where an airplane will depart depends upon how important it is to one that one know when and where the plane departs—whether one is to be on that plane, what will happen if one misses it, and so forth. Hawthorne and others suggest that this does not show that 'know' in different contexts of knowledge attribution denotes more or less stringent characteristics that beliefs have. Rather, it always denotes the single characteristic of constituting knowledge, which is simply harder for a belief to possess in some cases than others, and one of the factors that can make it harder for a belief to constitute knowledge is its importance to the possessor or others. I endorse Hawthorne's analysis of these cases, unsurprisingly, since I argued earlier that contextualism is false.

Now, such subject-dependence might very well depend on factors other than the importance of knowledge to a subject in the sense illustrated by the Bank Cases. Among those factors where testimonial knowledge is concerned might be whether the subject is a child. Perhaps it is easy for children to know that their parents know that that long-necked animal is a giraffe, and so to know themselves that that long-necked animal is a giraffe in accord with the KK view. It might be that their status as children—or more generally as subjects lacking much testimonial knowledge—is enough to make it easier to know that testifiers know. On the other hand, there are a number of reasons that can explain why this might be the case. The *kind* of propositions that children learn are perhaps particularly easy to know by testimony; it is easy to know for this reason that one's parents and teachers know much of what they know and testify to. A child's access to testifiers is largely confined to those who have his epistemic interests at heart. Perhaps this also makes it easier to know that those testifiers know, especially since much of their testimony will be confined by the testifiers themselves to sure-fire knowledge as opposed, for example, to unjustified speculation.

Once again, I stress, along Fricker's lines, that knowing that a testifier knows need not involve performing some kind of assessment of the testifier's testimony and of the testifier himself. In some cases, such knowledge might indeed demand such a thing, but in other cases it will not, and the testimonial knowledge acquired by children is likely to fall in the latter camp for the most part. Just as a somewhat externalist understanding of knowledge has it that we can often know propositions without having, and certainly without evaluating, explicit reasons for or against those propositions, we can take the same line toward second-order knowledge that others (or, for that matter, ourselves) know something. And that second-order knowledge, recall, will often be *implicit* knowledge—the testifee does not need to explicitly entertain the proposition that the testifier knows but merely have something like a disposition to do so in the right circumstances.

If we say that children can live up to the standards that the KK view demands, we do have to credit them with the *concept* of knowledge, of course, since they will know, and hence believe, propositions that employ that very concept concerning testifiers. Relatively young children certainly have such a concept; just how old they are when they acquire it is an empirical matter. I do not see a particular problem here for the KK view since even if children do acquire testimonial beliefs before they have the concept of knowledge, there is no obstacle to denying them knowledge at such an age for the coherentist reasons discussed above.

I will close by considering an objection to the KK view that differs from those considered thus far, the response to which suggests yet a *third* position on whether and how children acquire testimonial knowledge. A number of philosophers, inspired by Reid (1970), have considered the reception of testimonial beliefs comparable to the production of perceptual beliefs by the senses—there is something like a "faculty" for receiving testimonial beliefs just as there are faculties for producing perceptual beliefs (Plantinga 1993a, for example). Surely we are justified in our perceptual beliefs formed without reflection on the operation of our senses—equally, such beliefs often constitute knowledge, regardless of one's position on the relation between justification and knowledge. The KK view appears to impose much stronger requirements on testimonial knowledge than hold for perceptual knowledge, for which something like the BK view seems to be correct. All it takes to acquire knowledge from the operation of the senses in the right circumstances—the unexceptional circumstances that we occupy the vast majority of the time—is to believe what our senses tell us. Is it legitimate to treat testimonial and perceptual knowledge so differently?

My response is that I do not treat perceptual and testimonial knowledge differently in an unprincipled manner. If one's vision regularly encouraged one to form false beliefs about what the world outside one looks like because of defects internal to one's faculties, or if the world outside one regularly put obstacles in the path of one's forming true beliefs—if people regularly placed fake barns and robot animals and trompe l'oeuil paintings wherever one roamed—one would have to know that one's senses were reporting accurately in order to acquire perceptual knowledge from them. Something *analogous* to the KK view would hold of perceptual knowledge. Thankfully, we are not in such a position with respect to the senses—perceptual knowledge is easy to obtain the vast majority of the time. (So is knowledge that one's senses are performing normally in a given situation, although I do not want to suggest that such knowledge is required for forming perceptual knowledge in ordinary circumstances. Implicit knowledge that one's senses are performing normally might, nevertheless, be commonplace or even universal when we acquire perceptual knowledge—it need not require any notable cognitive effort or reflection.)

But we are in such a position with respect to testimony a lot of the time— at least as adults.[27] As already stressed, sometimes it is easy to know that a testifier knows—when he is telling one the time, for example—and knowing that he knows requires little if any cognitive effort beyond that required to believe that he knows (provided that he does know). On many other occasions, it is not so easy. In light of the differences between the testimonial environment of children and that of adults sketched above, perhaps we should consider the requirements for *children's* testimonial knowledge to be analogous to those holding for adults' *perceptual* knowledge, and not those holding for adults' testimonial knowledge. Even if it is a lot easier for children to know that testifiers know than it is for adults in light of the above discussion, perhaps we should say that it is nevertheless not required for children to know that the testifier knows in order to acquire testimonial knowledge. Perhaps for children (and those in comparable testimonial environments), the BK view holds—all they have to do is believe what they are told in order to know provided that the testifier himself knows.

Again, I am not going to take a firm view on the matter. Whatever we should say about children's testimonial knowledge, their knowledge or lack of it does not present a problem for holding that adults must meet the standard of the KK view in order to acquire testimonial knowledge. It is not a problem if children lack testimonial knowledge. It is not a problem if children have to meet the KK standard if they are to have testimonial knowledge—they plausibly can do so. And it is not a problem if children only have to meet a weaker standard than adults do to acquire testimonial knowledge. Children are, after all, rather different from adults, and it is not a problem to treat them so—even in epistemology.

3.5   Conclusion

One last point: we can solve a small philosophers' puzzle that is so small that it does not, perhaps, amount to a small *philosophical* puzzle. Philosophers are often wont to scratch their heads when "lay people" invoke the fact–opinion distinction. When testifiee tells testifier "that's your *opinion;* I want the facts," it is hard to make sense of the assertion, understanding 'fact' as philosophers tend to. One can perfectly well have an opinion, even a *mere* opinion (that is, an opinion that lacks justification), that corresponds to a fact; one can opine, even *merely* opine, a true proposition. To dismiss an opinion as an opinion as opposed to a fact and so, in some sense, a mere opinion is not, it seems, to claim that the opinion is false. Neither is it to claim that the opiner does not know what he opines. An assertion that does not express knowledge can be criticized on those grounds alone, but "that's your opinion" is not as strong a criticism, if any criticism at all, as "you don't know that." Rather, I suggest, to dismiss a proffered opinion as a mere opinion is more to say "*I* don't know that." That is, the testifiee cannot take you at your word since if he did derive a belief from your testimony that p, he would not know that p, and so his belief would be unjustified. The testifiee does not know that you know that p, and that is why what you say is just your opinion. To state a fact as opposed to an opinion, in this colloquial sense, is to make a statement from which one's audience can derive knowledge because your audience will know that you know what you are talking about.

4 Inference

4.1 Introduction

In this chapter, I will derive a general definition of "good" inference from the identification of justification and knowledge. I will then apply the definition to deductive and inductive inference, discussion of the latter occupying most of the chapter. I will argue that my view of good inference has no problem with denying that knowledge is closed under known logical implication ("closure"), as it appears not to be (and for reasons quite independent of skepticism). I will then argue that it is essential in general to distinguish "probabilistic" inferences, in which the conclusion is highly probable given the premises of the inference, from good inductive inferences proper. An inference can be bad no matter how high the probability of the conclusion given the premises (and "background knowledge"). Whether inductive inferences are nevertheless a proper subclass of probabilistic inferences is a matter on which I will remain neutral; it does not follow from the fact that inductive inferences are not deductive that they are probabilistic. I will derive a definition of the conditions under which some evidence is evidence *for* a hypothesis from the identification of justification and knowledge and argue that it handles some well-known problems that other theories of the evidence-for relation face. The success of the account of evidence given provides further support for the identification of justification and knowledge since it is a consequence of that view of justification.

4.2 Good Inference

I intend the term 'good' to express the most important epistemic virtue that an inference of any kind can have. It is tempting to suppose that if an inference is *deductive,* then it is good just in case it is sound; I will argue in the next section that this is incorrect and that a sound inference need not be good. However, soundness is surely the model for goodness in general in *one* sense. Just as a sound inference is one that has true premises and a conclusion that is entailed by those premises (the reasoning is valid), in general a good inference has good premises and good reasoning, the combination of which is reliably associated with a good conclusion.

This formulation is deliberately very vague and general to keep as many on board as possible at this stage; we cannot yet say that a good inference has good premises that *lead to* or *guarantee* a good conclusion via good reasoning since probabilistic inferences will seem to be a counterexample to some. By definition, there is a chance that a probabilistic inference will lead to a false conclusion. Some will feel that a probabilistic *inference* can be good, but a false conclusion cannot be good. Others will feel that a false conclusion can be good since a good conclusion is simply a *justified* conclusion and that which is justified can nevertheless be false; a good probabilistic inference always has a good conclusion although there is a chance that it is false. I will argue that no inferences are good in virtue of the conclusion having a high probability less than one given the premises *even* if the premises *make* the conclusion very likely to be true[1] and even for one who knows the premises—although there are certainly good inferences that are unsound.

What I mean by 'inference' is fundamentally a psychological process whereby one forms beliefs; inferences in my sense can be *expressed* in public language, but they occur in the mind. If one insists that, strictly speaking, an inference is something abstract that a psychological process itself at best expresses or bears some other relation to, I imagine that little of what I say will need anything but terminological modification. If one has that more abstract conception of inference, then one will, in any case, need to supplement it with some tie to the mind to consider the epistemological issues that will concern us—perhaps in the manner of Richard Feldman (1994, 179):

An argument is a good argument for a person S if and only if (i) S is justified in believing the conjunction of all the premises of the argument, (ii) S is justified in believing that the premises are "properly connected" to the conclusion, and (iii) the argument is not defeated for S.

What I will call 'an inference' is for Feldman a relation between an abstract argument and a person who himself stands in the belief relation to the propositional constituents of the argument. (Feldman is concerned with the [potential] public presentation of an argument rather than a psychological process inessentially related to any linguistic expression thereof. Despite this, there is no obvious impediment to considering his definition to apply equally to psychological processes.) I will follow Feldman (and orthodoxy) in taking premises and conclusions to be propositions (and hence, in some sense, abstracta) to which one is related when one engages in an inference. Taking *inferences* to be abstracta—formal propositional structures—is, of course, very useful if one is engaged in logical inquiry. If one is rather engaged in epistemological inquiry, it is less useful, especially if one is concerned with inductive inference since the very existence of inductive logic is highly questionable. Moreover, I will suggest that we should resist the temptation to identify good deductive inference with sound deductive argument as it figures in the unquestionably useful discipline of deductive logic; if we followed Feldman in conceiving of inferences (arguments) as abstracta, resisting the temptation is more of an uphill struggle.[2]

Some of the complexities of Feldman's definition can be removed if we talk of inference in the psychological sense. A good inference will result from a good argument only if the inferrer actually draws the conclusion of the good argument. One who infers a conclusion from premises necessarily takes there to be a connection between premises and conclusion, and we will suppose that he does so properly if and only if the reasoning in his inference is good. If someone happens to believe the premises of an argument in Feldman's sense and happens to believe the conclusion, the goodness of the argument still depends on him connecting the conclusion to the premises. His making an inference at all in our sense depends upon there being such a connection, and so we will not need a clause such as (ii) above in our definition of a good inference. Besides, (ii) itself is arguably not enough to do the job; the inferrer has to actually connect premises and conclusion, not merely believe, however justifiably, that there is a connection. Even if premises and conclusion are properly connected and the inferrer believes that they are, the good argument in Feldman's sense will lead to a good inference only if the inferrer *in fact* comes to believe the conclusion on the basis of that proper connection.

That aside, I have few problems with Feldman's account of a good argument for a person once it has been transformed into an account of good inference, instances of which are necessarily attached to persons (although he would have quite a few problems with my interpretation of his terms). What good is an inference if it does not result in justified beliefs? And could it be any good if it did not start from justified beliefs?[3] And what more could be required in a good inference than that the inferrer arrive at a justified belief by inferring it from justified beliefs? Of course, we need to say something about the good *reasoning* that is a proper part of a good inference and that can proceed from bad premises. What we have in that case, however, is *simply* good reasoning, not good inference *tout court,* in our sense of the notion. If the inferrer does not employ good reasoning to come to his conclusion, that will prevent his belief in the conclusion from being a justified one. Hence, since a good inference has a good conclusion by definition, we do not need explicitly to mention good reasoning in our definition of good inference. Nevertheless, how to characterize good reasoning, whether it proceeds from good or bad premises, is a question that I will return to below.

Feldman's (iii) suggests that something else is required to arrive at a good conclusion (that is, a justified belief): the argument must not be defeated. This condition is unnecessary on my conception of justified belief. Justified belief is knowledge. The premises of an inference are good, then, if they are known. If there were a defeater for *knowledge,* then the inferrer would not have made a good inference simply because he would not know the conclusion, its candidacy for knowledge having been defeated.[4] Conversely, there are subjects who *lack* the background knowledge that enables others to know a given conclusion by inferring it from known premises, although they know those premises from which others infer the conclusion. A psychological definition of good inference does not need any explicit reference to the background knowledge on which the goodness of an inference undoubtedly often depends since inferences in the psychological sense occur in a particular psychological context—performed by a particular subject at a particular time with whatever background knowledge he has at that time.[5] Another complexity of Feldman's definition that can be discarded is the reference to the inferrer's belief in the *conjunction* of the premises being justified since if the inferrer knows the premises individually, he can know their conjunction and arguably does know their conjunction at least implicitly. The possibility that justified belief is not closed under conjunction even if one forms a belief in the conjunction when one's beliefs in the conjuncts are all justified motivates Feldman's requirement of justified belief in the conjunction of the premises. Since knowledge is closed under conjunction in the relevant sense, we do not need this complexity in our definition.[6]

A good inference arrives at a justified belief in its conclusion; that is, the inferrer knows the conclusion.

An inference from premises $P_1, \ldots, P_n$ to a conclusion C is good if and only if the inferrer knows that $P_1, \ldots, P_n$ and comes to know that C by inferring it from those premises.

And it's as simple as that. Despite its simplicity, I will argue in this chapter that good inference so defined provides the basis for solving a couple of philosophical problems: whether or not knowledge is closed under known logical implication, and the nature of evidence. However, for other philosophical problems, the definition, although not an *impediment* to finding a solution, does little to facilitate one. Consider the new riddle of induction (Goodman 1983) (or one form of it, at least). Having observed a sufficient number of green emeralds, one can justifiably infer that all emeralds are green. All the observed green emeralds are grue—they have the property of being green if first observed before a future time t or blue if first observed after t—and yet one cannot justifiably infer that all emeralds are grue since that entails that they are blue if first observed after t. Why not? It is no real answer—although it is true—that one can *know* that all emeralds are green on the basis of observing (and hence knowing) that a sufficient number are, whereas one cannot know that all emeralds are grue on the basis of observing any number of grue emeralds (it is, after all, false that all emeralds are grue). This is simply to restate the explanandum, having identified justification with knowledge. What is wanted is an explanation of *how* we can know that all emeralds are green having observed a sufficient number of green emeralds even if the observed emeralds are also grue.

Perhaps a satisfactory answer cannot be given. Explaining how one can know a conclusion on the basis of known premises with any generality is, I suggest, quite similar to defining knowledge and holds at least as little chance of success. Indeed, it is hard to see how a fully general definition of good inference in more fundamental terms than my definition employs could fail implicitly to define knowledge. In a sense, defining knowledge itself can be seen as defining a 0-premise inference to a known conclusion, and we should not expect defining an n-premise inference from known premises to a known conclusion for $n > 0$ to be any easier. On the other hand, it is easier to say something illuminating about why some instances of *particular* kinds of beliefs (mathematical beliefs, beliefs about the future, beliefs about one's own mental states, etc.) constitute knowledge than to define knowledge in general, and it is presumably correspondingly easier to say something illuminating about why particular kinds of inference from known premises lead to known conclusions than to define good inference in general in more fundamental terms than I have. Perhaps the new riddle of induction presents a sufficiently particular question about good inference that we can hope for an answer, and perhaps not.[7]

My definition of good inference is perhaps *slightly* more helpful in considering inference to the best explanation (IBE). Is inference to the best explanation a fundamental inferential norm?[8] Well, in a sense, it clearly is not on my view of good inference. It doesn't matter how good an explanation theory T is of the evidence if one cannot know that T is true on the basis of that evidence and the fact that it explains the evidence and all the other relevant knowledge that one has—an inference that T is true will not be good. So the real question, perhaps, is: does the fact that a theory is the best explanation of the evidence enable one to know the theory, and is its being the best explanation in some sense fundamental to explaining why one knows the theory? My definition of good inference can perhaps help to clarify the question about IBE, even if it cannot help to answer it.

Good inference is, I suggest, not the *only* way to know something through inference. An inferential belief can be justified even if the inference that gave rise to it was not a good one because its premises were not good even if the *reasoning* from premises to conclusion was good.

I will give examples of such inferences after considering what good reasoning amounts to on my view. Good reasoning is reasoning that gives rise to knowledge when applied to knowledge, that leads from known premises to a known conclusion. This is our counterpart to validity in the definition of soundness in deductive logic. A valid inference *form* is such that the conclusion of any instance of the form is true *if* the premises are. A sound inference is valid (an instance of a valid form) and has true premises. Validity is defined in terms of "good" premises (although not in the sense relevant to us)—goodness is truth for propositions by the standards of deductive logic. Good reasoning in our sense is similarly defined in terms of the goodness of propositions; for us, for a proposition to be good, when serving as a premise in an inference, it has to be known by the inferrer. Reasoning is good just in case if its premises were known, its conclusion would also be known and on the basis of the knowledge of the premises. There are hence inferences that are not good because they do not employ good premises although they employ good reasoning; if they had also employed good premises, they would have been good inferences.

Now, our definition of good reasoning is imprecise, even half baked, compared to the definition of validity in deductive logic for at least two reasons. First, it is not formal; since it is to apply to inductive as well as deductive inferences and since there is little hope of a formal inductive logic, this is not a problem. It applies to token inferences directly, not in virtue of the properties of all token instances having the same form. When one token inference uses reasoning of the same type as another token inference is an imprecise, even context-sensitive matter; it is not a matter of precise and contextually invariant form. Second, given the counterfactual nature of our definition, it is likely that there are inferences that count as employing good reasoning by our definition that do not employ good reasoning in any remotely intuitive sense. Suppose that I in fact have a completely crazy belief from which I crazily infer an utterly crazy conclusion. It is not hard to imagine that there will be cases fitting this profile that are such that if I were to *know* what is in fact crazy for me to believe, then the world (including my mind and the beliefs that I have) would be sufficiently different that I could know the crazy conclusion on the basis of the actually crazy belief given, for example, the background knowledge that I would have in a world in which I could know what it is in fact crazy to believe.

To attempt to defend my vague definition of good reasoning confronted with such a case, the best bet would probably be to deny that I would be using the *same* reasoning in inferring the actually crazy conclusion from the actually crazy premise or premises were I to know the actually crazy premises. I will not attempt to construct such a counterexample in detail and *a fortiori* I will not attempt to construct such a defense. The *real* response to this worry is to shrug one's shoulders and say that it is the notion of good inference that is the important one, not the notion of good reasoning, which is little more than a vague derivative of the definition of good inference. Reasoning is good reasoning if it would be part of a good inference were the premises good. This is vague and problematic as counterfactual definitions tend to be, but we do not need anything more precise since it is primarily good inference that concerns us.

We can ask of any proposition at all, true or false, known or unknown, what its deductive consequences are and at least sketch an answer to that question with relative ease. It is partially a purely formal matter—it follows from the proposition that the moon is red that something is red—and partially a matter of meaning—it follows from the proposition that the moon is red that the moon is colored.[9] We cannot ask of any given proposition what its inductive consequences are. What inductive inferences could we draw from the proposition that the moon is red? One is at a loss to answer this question, and it does not help to ask what we could know (or justifiably believe, if one draws a distinction) on the basis of knowing (or justifiably believing) that the moon is red. It depends heavily on what one's background knowledge would be, what the world would be like if the moon were red, and so on, and, given the nonexistence of a formal inductive logic, there is no hope of answering such questions in a systematic fashion. Consequently, trying to distill a rigorous notion of good reasoning from our definition of good inference in order to apply it to inferences that lack good premises is ill motivated.

And yet, I want to suggest, it is possible to acquire inferential beliefs that constitute knowledge and yet do not arise from *good* inferences since they do not arise from good premises. An example that I take from Hawthorne (2004) is that of children who infer that they will receive gifts on Christmas Day on the basis of their false belief that Santa Claus will visit on Christmas Eve. I agree with Hawthorne that it is plausible that such children know that they will receive presents on Christmas Day even though their belief that they will is inferred from a false belief. Another example that Hawthorne presents is of a person who falsely believes that a particular individual is under four feet tall when he is in fact an inch over (we can suppose that he arrives at this belief by observation); nevertheless, he knows that the individual is short by inference from his false belief. A quite different example (not taken from Hawthorne) is provided by people who believe false but practically reliable scientific theories. A belief in Newtonian mechanics enables one to know how the physical world will behave in many respects despite the falsity of one's Newtonian beliefs.[10] We should not classify these inferences as good inferences since their premises are unjustified; nevertheless, they do yield knowledge.[11]

4.3 Closure

There has been a lot of discussion in recent decades of whether knowledge is closed under known logical implication. If one knows that p and one knows that if p then q, then can one know that q with great ease by simply inferring that q via the simple and valid rule of *modus ponens (MP)*, for all propositions p and q?[12] There are at least two classes of alleged counterexamples to the claim that one can do so without exception. (None question that one can do so in many cases; knowledge is closed under known logical implication *almost* without exception.) One concerns propositions that express skeptical possibilities.[13] As G. E. Moore said, we know that we have hands. And we know that if we have hands, then we are not disembodied brains in vats subjected to hallucinations that we have hands. So, if closure holds, then we know, or can know with great ease, that we are not brains in vats, and likewise for all similar skeptical possibilities. Or we do not know that we have hands after all. Some, following Nozick, have claimed that we know that we have hands and do not know that we are not brains in vats despite also knowing the conditional premise of an *MP* inference—closure fails. A number of suggested definitions of knowledge, such as Nozick's, have precisely this consequence.[14]

The other class of alleged counterexamples is of a much more quotidian nature. Jonathan Vogel (1990) calls them "Car Theft Cases." I know that my car is parked on Not Utterly Safe St. And I know that if my car is parked on that street, then it has not been stolen. If closure holds, I can know with great ease that my car has not been stolen. But it seems that I can know no such thing, although I might very well know that my car has probably not been stolen (if I could not even know *that*, perhaps I could not know where my car is parked). There are numerous quotidian cases conforming to this pattern. Perhaps it is even the case that almost all contingent knowledge entails propositions that it seems that we do not know and infinitely many of them; although for each of them, it is plausible to suppose that we know (or could know upon minimal reflection, having explicitly entertained the relevant proposition) that it is very likely that the proposition is true.[15] It is less intuitive to claim that we know that we are very likely not brains in vats but do not know categorically that we are not; we either categorically know that we are not brains in vats, or categorically know no such thing. I will not discuss skepticism any further (although what I say concerning closure might well be useful in such a discussion); the car theft cases are my main concern.[16]

Why do so many philosophers consider the failure of closure to be so implausible? Certainly, applications of *modus ponens* had better yield knowledge in the circumstances when that rule of inference is actually followed if we are to know much of what we think we know, but since people do not actually infer that their cars have not been stolen on the basis of their beliefs about where they are parked (although they do tend to believe, and in general know, that their cars have *probably* not been stolen), a denial of closure in the cases in question will not lead to a damaging skepticism about a good deal of quotidian knowledge. Rather, a great deal of the appeal that closure has derives from the appeal that *modus ponens* has. *Modus ponens* is a valid rule of inference; necessarily, its conclusion is true if the premises are. Not only that, it is a simple and unquestionably epistemically basic rule of inference. All adult humans who are remotely close to normal cognitive functioning can, and at least implicitly do, grasp it and could not form a fraction of the beliefs that they do form if they did not grasp it. It is natural, then, to suppose that *modus ponens* could not be anything other than a good inference rule, a rule all of whose instances are good inferences if the premises are good.

A natural, but questionable supposition. Good inference in general cannot be a matter of soundness since there are good inductive inferences. No one who is not an inductive skeptic fails to recognize this fact, of course, but if one starts with the idea that instances of valid forms of inference with known premises are the *best* inferences since those instances always preserve truth, it is natural to think that instances of forms of inference that *almost* always preserve truth with known premises are only a bit worse but still good, and that instances of forms of inference that preserve truth most of the time with known premises are, well, not bad. If, on the other hand, one grounds one's conception of good inference in *knowledge* preservation (or, more generally, in justification preservation however one conceives of justification) at the outset, then whether *modus ponens* is a form of inference all of whose instances with known premises are good depends upon whether all of its instances preserve knowledge. To suppose that *modus ponens* applied to known premises is the acme of good inference from the outset begs the question in favor of closure. The car theft cases (and, for some, the skeptical cases) suggest that *modus ponens* is not the acme of good inference despite being truth preserving. Truth preservation is one thing, a central concern of deductive logic (which I am not impugning in the slightest), and good inference is another. Perhaps conjunction introduction applied to known premises is the acme of good inference, all inferences of the form p, q, so p & q preserving knowledge, but *modus ponens* is not.[17]

4.4 Probabilistic Inferences

The known unknown beliefs are not justified. Since this is so, the following two inferences performed by one who knows the premises are not good, even for those who take good inference to be a matter of *justification* preservation and do not identify knowledge and justification.

1. 95 percent of basketball players are tall.
2. Bill is a basketball player.
3. So, Bill is tall.

1. I have just one ticket in a fair lottery.
2. There are a million tickets in the lottery.
3. So, my ticket will lose the lottery.

On the other hand, the following two inferences are good as performed by one who knows the premises, at least if he has the appropriate background knowledge or, more saliently, lacks inappropriate background knowledge.

1. 95 percent of basketball players are tall.
2. Bill is a basketball player.
3. So, there is a 95 percent chance that Bill is tall.

1. I have just one ticket in a fair lottery.
2. There are a million tickets in the lottery.
3. So, my ticket will probably lose the lottery.

(Numeric precision can be added to the second inference and removed from the first, and the transformed inference will, of course, remain good as performed by one who knows the premises.)[18]

The inferences in the first set are probabilistic inferences. Their conclusions have a probability strictly less than one given their premises.[19] The inferences in the second set are not probabilistic in any straightforward sense by that definition. Whether *good* inductive inferences are probabilistic in any sense, I will address below.

One cannot know the conclusions of the first set of inferences by inferring them from the premises. One can know the conclusions of the second set by inferring them from the premises—*ceteris paribus*. If one knows that a ticket with the first nine digits the same as one's own ten-digit ticket won, for example, one cannot know the conclusion of the second inference by inferring it from the premises. Neither could one know that there is a 95 percent chance that Bill is tall by inferring that conclusion from one's knowledge that 95 percent of basketball players are tall and that Bill is a basketball player if one also knew that Bill had given a talk about his being a short basketball player. To deny that probabilistic inferences such as those in the first set are good does not, contra Feldman (1994, 183), "make the notion of a good nondeductive argument useless." There are good inductive inferences whose conclusions are not explicitly probabilistic, unlike those in the second set of inferences. That the truth of one's premises is consistent with the falsity of one's conclusion does not prevent one from knowing the conclusion by inferring it from the premises. If one knows enough instances of a generalization, then one can in *many* cases know that the generalization is true by inferring it from the instances, depending on one's background knowledge—what else one knows. If one knows of slightly fewer instances, the best one can know in many cases is that the generalization is very probably true. Inductive inferences are often assimilated to probabilistic inferences simply because neither are deductive; unless one sloppily uses 'probabilistic' as a synonym for 'inductive', this assimilation is questionable. All probabilistic inferences such as those in the first set above are bad; some inductive inferences are good. At best, inductive inferences are a proper subset of probabilistic inferences, a matter I will discuss in more detail below.

The main assumption that encourages the use of the term 'probabilistic' to mean 'inductive' is the assumption that the conclusion of a nondeductive inference always has a particular probability strictly less than one given its premises, and the higher it is, the better the inference—a nondeductive inference is always probabilistic. (We will not address the question of whether the inferences in the second set are deductive or not.) A further consequence of my view of good inference (and, more generally, of the view that the known unknown beliefs are unjustified) is that the goodness of an inductive inference cannot be explained informatively in terms of the premises of the inference making the conclusion probable, or probable to at least some fixed or contextually determined degree. Inferences to the conclusion that one's ticket will not win a fair lottery are never good no matter how many tickets there are since one never knows that one's ticket will not win a fair lottery before the drawing is made. In general, no matter how probable one's conclusion is given one's premises (at least if it is strictly less than one), the goodness of one's inference is not assured since there will be a bad lottery-inference exhibiting the same probabilities. If one insisted that there is a probability such that if the conclusion had that probability given the goodness of the premises, then the inference is good, that probability would have to be one so that no lottery inference would present a counterexample. It is a short step from here to concluding that a proposition p has probability one for a person just in case he knows that p, a position that Williamson (2000, ch. 9) endorses. Inductive inferences would not be probabilistic inferences, all of the latter being bad. An alternative position is that probability and good inference have no simple or theoretically interesting relationship.[20] Perhaps for any large enough probability still strictly less than one, there are good inferences whose conclusions have that probability given their premises, even though there are also bad inferences, such as lottery inferences, with the same characteristic (although their premises are good, since known). I will remain neutral on which of these views is correct.

The notion of a *comparatively* good inference makes no sense on my view of good inference, at least strictly speaking, any more than does the notion of the *degree* of justification that a belief has. However, as we explained in section 2.3, even though beliefs that are more or less tentative in their probabilistic contents are justified to the same degree if they are justified at all, someone who knows that it is extremely likely that p (but not categorically that p) can be said to have "more justification for believing that p" than someone who merely knows that it is fairly likely that p in a perfectly practical, colloquial, and nonfundamental sense of 'justification' (although, as we stressed, it is perhaps more 'belief' that has the relevant colloquial usage). Similarly, *perhaps* an inference that is, strictly speaking, a good inference and that is the best I can do on the matter of whether or not p to the proposition that it is extremely likely that p can be described in a loose, perfectly serviceable, and nonfundamental sense of 'good inference' as not "as good an inference" as a good inference categorically to p, just as my inference can be loosely described as better than that of an inferrer whose only good inference is to the proposition that it is *quite* likely that p. Probability has a role in clarifying the nature of good inference, but it is not that of explaining the *relation* between premises and conclusion. It is that of clarifying the conclusion; what is loosely described as inferring that p is often strictly speaking an inference to the conclusion that probably *p* (or something similar), just as what is strictly speaking a belief that probably *p* (and often a justified belief) is often loosely described as a belief that *p*.

4.5 Evidence

Both epistemologists and epistemologically oriented philosophers of science use the term 'evidence' extensively, although their usage is perplexingly dissonant. What evidence amounts to, and which beliefs or believed propositions count as evidence, is a matter of great controversy in the philosophy of science. Many epistemologists, on the other hand, use the term as though what constitutes a believer's evidence is itself self-evident. Just as it was once popular to regard one's evidence as what is "given"—one's *data* in the most etymologically appropriate sense, that to which the greatest certainty attaches—one almost gets the impression that the *concept* of evidence and the extension thereof is regarded as a given in much epistemology.[21]

It is no comfort to suppose that philosophers of science and epistemologists are largely concerned with distinct notions—the epistemologists with evidence *simpliciter* and the philosophers of science with the notion of evidence *for* a hypothesis. There is some truth to that claim, although many philosophers of science talk of evidence *simpliciter* and many epistemologists of one's evidence for a certain proposition or propositions—and the latter usage is generally as blasé as much talk of evidence *simpliciter*. However, it would be rather implausible to suggest that evidence *simpliciter* is *independent* of the evidence-for relation. Rather, it is simply defined in terms of that relation: something counts as an element of one's unqualified evidence just in case it is evidence for *something or other*.[22] The evidence-for relation is fundamental, and philosophers of science are right to take its extension as far from obvious. That relation will be the focus of this section.

The blasé usage of 'evidence' by epistemologists perhaps has a counterpart vice within the philosophy of science. If *e* is evidence for a hypothesis *h*, then if *e* is *my* evidence, it constitutes a "good reason" for believing *h*, as Achinstein (2001) stresses—it justifies belief in that hypothesis. The extension of 'justified belief' is at least as controversial for epistemologists as that of 'evidence' is for philosophers of science, and this book adds to that controversy far from inconsiderably. 'Justified belief' is perhaps thrown around by some philosophers of science with as much abandon as 'evidence' is within epistemology. Neither notion provides an Archimedean point for understanding the other, *pace* the (mutually contrary) assumptions that some epistemologists and some philosophers of science seem to make. Although I disavow both those assumptions, having thus far sided with epistemologists in taking the notion of justification very much not for granted, I will be siding with the philosophers of science more than the epistemologists in discussing evidence. The view of the evidence-for relation defended in this section stands evidentialism, the view that justification and/or knowledge is a matter of having proper evidential support for one's beliefs (Feldman and Conee 1985), on its head.[23] Rather than explicating knowledge and justification in terms of evidence, I will explicate evidence in terms of justification (and, hence, knowledge). To do so, having sorted out what justification amounts to, is to stand on firmer ground than the evidentialist and many fellow travelers among epistemologists who take the extension of the concept of evidence to be relatively unproblematic.

Evidence e for a hypothesis h justifies belief in h, then. So, I should be able to infer h from e—that inference ought to be a good one if my evidence is itself good. Since good evidence should constitute the premises of a good inference to that for which it is evidence, I follow Williamson in taking evidence to be knowledge.[24] (Williamson takes *all* knowledge to be evidence, a position I will not endorse, although I am not unsympathetic to his claim.) Even if one wishes to take evidence to be merely a proposition or propositions, one will need an account of what it is to *have* that evidence, and even if one does not identify justification with knowledge as I do, one might nevertheless restrict at least the evidence one possesses to what one knows. As with the distinction between inferences and Feldman's arguments, the two ways of talking about evidence, although they reflect underlying philosophical differences (in particular, whether one can, and should, talk of evidential relations between one proposition and another regardless of whether either proposition is known by anyone, a matter that I will discuss at the end of the chapter), *in themselves* do not clearly differ more than terminologically. Now, if a good inference is one that yields knowledge of its conclusion inferred from knowledge of its premises, as I have argued is a fairly straightforward consequence of the identification of justification and knowledge, it seems that I will also have to say that e is evidence for h just in case one can know h by inferring it from e.[25] (Since this conception of evidence is based on a psychological notion of good inference, the evidence-for relation must be relativized at least implicitly to inferrers themselves: if an inferrer I could know that h by inferring it from e, then e is evidence for h for I. If he actually makes the inference, then perhaps we should say that e *was* evidence for h for I.)[26]

Even if I have successfully defended the identification of justification and knowledge to this point, surely, the reader might very well say, I cannot endorse *that* claim. And, the reader might well add, it casts serious doubt on—perhaps even refutes—the identification of justification and knowledge since it is hard to see how I can avoid endorsing that claim.

On the contrary, I will argue that this simple account of the "evidence-for" relation supports the identification of justification and knowledge since it gives a satisfying account of some puzzle cases concerning evidence in a very effective manner. *Supports?* What does that mean if not that the simple account of the evidence-for relation enables one to *know* that justified belief is knowledge—by the simple account's own lights! It is time for:

4.5.1 The Bit Where You Take It Back, Part III

Even though there is a fundamental distinction between believing that p and believing that probably p, I argued in section 2.3 that in colloquial speech, 'belief that p' often denotes mere belief that probably p as well as categorical belief that p. This is not true of 'knowledge that p'; it cannot be used colloquially to denote mere knowledge that probably p. Ignoring terminological issues concerning the exact relation between evidence and propositions, all evidence is knowledge, and all knowledge might well be evidence, but 'evidence' is not 'knowledge', and I suggest that the term behaves more like 'belief' than 'knowledge'—it has the characteristics typical of 'belief' to an even greater degree than 'belief' itself, in fact.

Fundamentally, we need to distinguish evidence that h from evidence that probably h, and, even more so, from evidence that there is at least a small chance that h. In practice, 'evidence that h' can be used perfectly serviceably to denote evidence that h, mere evidence that probably h, or even mere evidence that there is at least a small chance that h. Whether the last of the three possible denotations is appropriate rather depends on the pragmatic context, as we will see below. Similarly, practically speaking, someone can be said to have *stronger* evidence for a hypothesis than someone else who nevertheless has evidence for the hypothesis. Strictly speaking, this is a matter of the two having equally good evidence for stronger and weaker hypotheses: evidence that it is somewhat likely that h as opposed to evidence that it is very likely that h, or evidence that it is very likely that h as opposed to categorical evidence that h, numerically precise counterparts of such hypotheses, and so on.[27]

The colloquial usage of 'evidence' is, I suggest, a huge problem when engaged in by philosophers. The philosophical literature on evidence by and large does not distinguish between evidence that h and evidence that probably h; this is the source of many of the philosophical problems that surround evidence. Strictly speaking, e can be evidence for probably h and not evidence for h since, often, one can know that probably h by inferring it from e (if one has appropriate background knowledge) but cannot know categorically that h by such an inference. And when we do epistemology (and epistemological philosophy of science), we should speak strictly when it matters. If we confuse the ephemeral and relatively undisciplined with what is fundamental and disciplined, we are likely to engage in complex and endless debate. As it goes with the epistemological literature on justification, so it goes with the literature on evidence, and for very similar reasons.

(Of course, sometimes we should speak *loosely* when it matters, even in epistemology. In many cases, it would be pedantic to distinguish evidence that h from evidence that probably h, and increase verbosity while decreasing clarity—particularly if one speaks of evidence in the earlier parts of a book most of whose readers are not accustomed to drawing the distinction and have not yet reached the later parts of that same book where the distinction is made and argued for. I spoke loosely in section 1.2.1 when I talked of the Gettier victim having "such good evidence" that he had a colleague who owned a Ford. Strictly speaking, he merely had evidence that his colleague *probably* owned a Ford. Likewise, someone unaware that he is in the land of fake barns has knowledge of how things look that does not, strictly speaking, amount to evidence that there is a barn in the middle distance—it merely amounts to evidence that there *probably* is. Someone outside the land of fake barns might well have knowledge of identical propositions about how things look that does amount, strictly speaking, to evidence that there is a barn in the middle distance. Knowledge of the very same propositions is evidence for the barn "hypothesis" *strictly speaking* for the one individual and merely loosely speaking for the other.)

What goes for 'evidence' goes for 'support', 'confirmation', and similar notions. Evidence confirms or supports a theory, strictly speaking, if one can know the theory to be true on the basis of the evidence, which is itself knowledge (or at least known, depending upon our terminology). Speaking more loosely, the evidence merely has to enable one to infer that the theory is *probably* true for it to support or confirm the theory. Speaking even more loosely, the evidence or *reasons* offered for believing a view are good reasons, they support the view, if they enable one to know that there is at least some chance that the view is correct—how much of a chance and how it relates to how much of a chance of being true that one knew that the view had before being supplied with those reasons, is, I suggest, context sensitive. It was in an appropriate context that I asserted (or at least tried to assert) that how my view of evidence handles problem cases for evidence supports the identification of justification and knowledge. Strictly speaking, it does no such thing—how it handles the problem cases is nowhere near enough for one to know that justified belief is knowledge. The *positive relevance* view of evidence, according to which e is evidence for h just in case $P(h|e) > P(h)$, captures at best an important factor in what makes a context appropriate for asserting that something is evidence for a theory loosely speaking even if it is not evidence in, we might say, the strict sense.

(Everyone should acknowledge at least a loose usage of 'evidence' that does not imply that one has good reasons for believing the hypothesis for which there is said to be evidence—a usage that, indeed, implies that there are *not* such reasons. For one can say that the evidence for a hypothesis h is *weak* and that the evidence for not-h is much stronger. 'Weak' is not a term like 'fake'—fake evidence is simply not evidence at all, whereas weak evidence *is* evidence in some sense. If one had absolutely conclusive evidence for not-h—if one knew that not-h—then one would not have even weak evidence for h. One would have no evidence at all for h, even if one would have had weak evidence for h had one possessed, at best, evidence that *most probably* not-h, strictly speaking. When one has merely weak evidence for h, one has, strictly speaking, merely evidence that there is at least some chance that h. If one knew that not-h, one would not have evidence that there was any chance that h, speaking strictly or loosely. The acquisition of weak evidence for a hypothesis might well, of course, mark the start of a process of evidence accumulation that terminates with the acquisition of evidence for the hypothesis *strictly speaking*—when one is in a position to know the hypothesis to be true on the basis of one's evidence.)

As with the case of 'belief' (section 2.3), I am not endorsing the claim that 'evidence' is ambiguous between a strict sense and a looser sense that is defined disjunctively in terms of the strict sense as evidence$_{strict}$ that p or evidence$_{strict}$ that probably p or (depending on contextual factors) evidence$_{strict}$ that there is at least a small chance that p. Perhaps evidence in the strict sense is strictly speaking the only sense that 'evidence' has, but the assertion that e is evidence for a hypothesis h might, although false, communicate a truth in a pragmatically acceptable fashion. On the other hand, I am quite open to the possibility that the *converse* is true, that there is no sense of 'evidence' corresponding to my strict sense (except as the term is used in this chapter), strictly speaking. Perhaps the only sense of 'evidence' is my so-called loose sense of the term. In that case, we can define an epistemologically more fundamental notion in terms of which evidence proper can be defined—call it 'evidence*'. 'Evidence*' is defined in terms of knowledge exactly as 'evidence' "in the strict sense" was earlier. 'Evidence' in its normal, and perhaps only, sense can be defined disjunctively in terms of evidence* in the obvious way. Whether there is a sense of 'evidence' outside of this book in which it denotes evidence* is not very important. *As far as epistemology is concerned,* there should be.

I do not propose to go into the contextual factors that make an assertion about evidence in the loose sense appropriate, or to give any account of the linguistic context-dependence of the colloquial use of 'evidence' since *evidence* (or at least evidence*) is not context-sensitive in this way, and it is evidence, not 'evidence' in its colloquial sense, that matters. The semantic and pragmatic factors involved are not relevant to evidence in the fundamental sense, and so not of great epistemological interest. The positive relevance conception of evidence is incorrect for evidence in the fundamental sense since even if one were to come to know that the first nine digits of the ten-digit winning number in the lottery match those on one's own ticket, one would still not know that one has won the lottery even though P(that I have won the lottery|My ticket has the first nine digits of the winning number)) $\gg P$(that I have won the lottery). If that does come to be my evidence (i.e., I come to know that I have the first nine numbers right), all I can infer (*ceteris paribus*) is that I now have a good chance of having won the lottery (and my probability function is updated accordingly on a Bayesian view if I am "rational").[28] The high probability conception of evidence according to which e is evidence for h just in case $P(h|e) > 0.5$ is even more glaringly inconsistent with my view since I do not have any evidence that I have not won a fair lottery simply because I have just one ticket, strictly speaking; I have evidence that it is extremely likely that I have not won. Probability has a role to play in giving a complete account of when e is evidence for h but, as with justified belief *per se*, its proper place (in many cases) is as a part of the hypothesis for which one has evidence, not in the relation between the evidence and the hypothesis.

Something similar is very likely to be true for any of the many (actual and possible) elaborations of the basic probabilistic definitions of evidence that, in unadorned simplicity, are less popular than they used to be. Definitions of evidence with ever-increasing complexity added to handle problem cases have a tendency to proliferate much as definitions of knowledge did in response to Gettier problems. Given what was said in section 4.2 above, this is unsurprising. Attempting to define evidence in terms more fundamental than knowledge is similar to attempting to define good inference in such terms, a task that I suggested is no easier than attempting to define knowledge itself. On the other hand, as stated back in section 2.5, failed definitions of knowledge are far from uniformly *useless;* they give an account of important kinds of fact in which knowledge partially consists much of the time. Failed definitions of evidence, from Carnap's and Hempel's work onward, can be seen in a very similar light; perhaps Achinstein's definition in terms of explanatory connections to be considered shortly is one such. They give an account of important kinds of fact in which the goodness of an inference from evidence to hypothesis (that is, from knowledge to knowledge) partially consists much of the time. Just as I do not want to *rule out* the possibility of defining knowledge in the traditional manner, I do not want to rule out the possibility of some definition of evidence more fundamental than my own that is nevertheless *consistent* with it—a definition of my definition, in effect. But I am skeptical that such a possibility can be realized.

4.5.2 The Problem Cases

I will discuss Achinstein's well-known problem cases for the positive relevance and high probability views of evidence in their latest presentation (Achinstein 2001). I do so partially because his problems can be solved quite easily by my view of evidence and also because Achinstein's own theory of

evidence *in a (very limited) sense* anticipates my own—as one very important footnote in Achinstein's account shows. In some ways, Achinstein's
motivating goals are better satisfied by my theory than by his. I will only
discuss his theory in enough detail to illustrate how this is so. The discussion of Achinstein's problem cases also serves to demonstrate how my view
of evidence works in practice quite apart from its connection to his view.

The first two counterexamples purport to show that the positive relevance definition
fails to provide a sufficient condition for evidence.

(i) *First lottery counterexample*

b: On Monday all 1000 tickets in a lottery were sold, of which John bought 100 and
Bill bought 1. One ticket was drawn at random on Wednesday.

e: On Tuesday, all the lottery tickets except those of John and Bill were destroyed,
and on Wednesday one of the remaining tickets was drawn at random.

h: Bill won. (Achinstein 2001, 69)

Here, '*b*' is the (relevant) background knowledge that one has, '*e*' the evidence, and '*h*' the hypothesis. (Just as I need not explicitly mention background knowledge in my definition of good inference since I conceive of
inference psychologically, I do not, unlike Achinstein, need explicitly to
mention it in my definition of the evidence-for relation that is based upon
that definition of good inference. Once again, this is largely a terminological
matter.)

Diagnosis: Although the positive relevance definition entails that *e* is
evidence that Bill won since the destruction of the tickets not owned by
Bill and John would vastly increase the chances of Bill winning and so
$P(h|e) \gg P(h)$, Achinstein contends that *e* is evidence that *John* won, not
Bill, since his chance of winning is very high after the ticket destruction
unlike Bill's.

On my view, *e* would be evidence (if one knew *b*) that Bill has a 1 in
100 chance of winning and also evidence that he has a 10 times greater
chance of winning than he used to have. (*Would* be evidence since it
only *is* evidence if one actually knows *e*. I will address the possibilities
of a more expansive notion of evidence that includes any proposition in
the realm of evidence whether known or not as well as whether I can,
or should, explicitly incorporate background knowledge into my account
of evidence below. Would-be evidence is not an important notion, I will
claim, and so I will not worry about the problems that counterfactuals

present since I will use the notion of would-be evidence for expository purposes only. What we are really discussing is a hypothetical case in which a typical inferrer in typical circumstances actually does know e and b, and we are interested in for what hypotheses e is evidence for our hypothetical inferrer. I will largely drop the counterfactual qualification in diagnoses of the rest of the cases, although the reader should bear in mind that it [or a more precise hypothetical condition] is implicitly present.) Those two propositions (among others) one can know by inference from e given appropriate background knowledge (b in particular). The positive relevance definition is correct loosely speaking at best (and we do not care just who is loosely right *loosely* speaking). One cannot know h by inferring it from e. So e is not evidence for h, strictly speaking, just as Achinstein says.

But it is not evidence that John won, either. The best one can know by inference from e (given relevant background knowledge such as b) is that John has a 100 in 101 chance of winning, not that he will win; one can also know that he has a very good chance of winning, that he will probably win, and that there is at least a small chance that he will win. e would be evidence for all those hypotheses. It is not, contra Achinstein, evidence that John won. As in the cases to follow, my view of evidence agrees with some of Achinstein's quite intuitive claims about what is and is not evidence, but not others. It is somewhat intuitive that e is not evidence that Bill won *pace* the positive relevance definition—although it is also somewhat intuitive to say that e is evidence that Bill won. In the *loose* sense of evidence, it is a context-sensitive matter whether evidence in the strict sense that there is at least some chance considerably under 50 percent that p can be termed evidence that p.

On the other hand, in the loose sense, evidence that probably p can always be described simply as evidence that p. Because of this fact, it is not terribly intuitive to say that e is not evidence that John won in the strict sense, as I do. The use of the term 'evidence', together with 'confirm, 'support', and so on, is very much conditioned by a tradition that does not distinguish between belief that p and belief that probably p as strictly as it should and by a tradition that distinguishes justification from knowledge when it should not. My strict notion of evidence is not likely to be found intuitive by those influenced by such a tradition. But it is intuitive that evidence for a hypothesis provides a good reason to believe the hypothesis, as Achinstein stresses, and it is a very short path to my strict conception of evidence once one abandons the idea that justification, in any important sense, differs from knowledge.[29] In any case, my argument for my strict conception is not that it is intuitive; it is that it gives satisfying and consistent diagnoses of the problem cases, together with the fact that it follows from the identification of justification and knowledge for which I have already argued.

(ii) *A swimming counterexample*

b: Steve is a member of the Olympic swimming team who was in fine shape Wednesday morning.

e: On Wednesday, Steve was doing training laps in the water.

h: On Wednesday, Steve drowned. (Achinstein 2001, 70)

Diagnosis: On the positive relevance definition, $P(h|e) \gg P(h)$. I have no bones to pick with Achinstein here; that Steve was swimming is not evidence that he drowned on my view. It is evidence that there was a very small chance that he drowned. And it is evidence that he is more likely to have drowned than was the case before he went swimming. And in certain contexts, *that general pattern* might very well make claims analogous to the claim that Steve was swimming is evidence that Steve drowned perfectly acceptable *if one is speaking loosely*, although in no ordinary context is a claim precisely like this one likely to be intuitive.

Now for Achinstein's examples that are supposed to show that the positive relevance definition does not state *necessary* conditions for evidential support:

(iii) *Second lottery counterexample*

e_1: *The New York Times* reports that Bill Clinton owns all but one of the 1000 lottery tickets sold in a lottery.

e_2: *The Washington Post* reports that Bill Clinton owns all but one of the 1000 lottery tickets sold in a lottery.

b: This is a fair lottery in which one ticket drawn at random will win.

h: Bill Clinton will win the lottery. (Achinstein 2001, 70)

Diagnosis: In this case, the difference between a propositional conception of evidence-for and a psychological good inference conception of evidence-for is glaring. Achinstein's case against the positive relevance definition is that $P(h|e_1 \,\&\, e_2 \,\&\, b) = P(h|e_1 \,\&\, b)$, and so e_2 is not evidence for h given e_1 and b on the positive relevance definition; but e_2 is at least as good evidence for h as e_1, and both e_1 and e_2 are pretty good evidence for h.

On my view, neither piece of evidence nor their conjunction is evidence for h but at best for the claim that it is very likely that h, and its precise numeric counterpart; call such a claim h'. If one has *already* inferred h' from e_1 (and one retains that knowledge), then an inference from e_2 to h' is psychologically bizarre if not impossible; it is of no interest to ask whether this inference is nevertheless good. If one has not inferred h' (or one has forgotten it), then an inference to h' from e_2, or from e_1 & e_2 (or from e_1 a second time—or an nth time if one has forgotten h' $n{-}1$ times) is a good inference since one will know h' on that basis. Consequently, e_2 (or *knowledge* of e_2 since e_2 is merely a proposition) is indeed evidence for h' for many subjects.

(iv) *Intervening cause counterexample*

e_1: On Monday at 10 A.M. David, who has symptoms S, takes medicine M to relieve S.

e_2: On Monday at 10:15 A.M. David takes medicine M' to relieve S.

b: Medicine M is 95% effective in relieving S within 2 hours; medicine M' is 90% effective in relieving S within 2 hours, but has fewer side-effects. When taken within 20 minutes of having taken M medicine M' completely blocks the causal efficacy of M without affecting its own.

h: David's symptoms are relieved by noon on Monday. (Achinstein 2001, 71)

Diagnosis: Achinstein's claim is that e_2 is evidence for h even though $P(h|e_1$ & e_2 & $b) < P(h|e_1$ & $b)$, and so it is not evidence by the positive relevance definition. On my view, neither e_1 nor e_2 is evidence for h strictly speaking, although either, loosely speaking, could be said to be so for appropriate inferrers since from each one can infer in the right circumstances that there is a good chance that David's symptoms are relieved by noon on Monday; call that claim h'. If someone has already inferred h' from e_1, to *retain* knowledge that h' upon learning e_2, the inferrer will have to infer h' once more from e_2.[30] An inference from (knowledge of) e_1 to h' is good, and so e_1 is evidence for h', provided that the inferrer is not aware of e_2 *(ceteris paribus)*; otherwise, only e_2 is evidence for h'. The mere *fact* that David took M' does not undermine one's knowledge of e_1, and nor does it undermine one's knowledge that there is a 95 percent chance that his symptoms will be relieved by noon should one so infer *provided* that one is unaware of e_2. If one becomes aware of e_2, then one's *specific* inferential knowledge is undermined, although one's knowledge of e_1 is retained, as is one's knowledge of the less specific h' if one makes a new inference from e_2 (or, perhaps more accurately, one's knowledge of h' is momentarily lost but immediately restored by an unproblematic inference).

Achinstein's final counterexample targets the high probability rather than positive relevance definition of evidence:

(v) *Irrelevant information counterexample.*

e: Michael Jordan eats wheaties.

b: Michael Jordan is a male basketball star.

h: Michael Jordan will not become pregnant. (Achinstein 2001, 71)

Diagnosis: $P(h|e \& b) > \frac{1}{2}$ but e is not evidence for h, Achinstein says (and I agree). On my good inference conception of evidence, if someone could come to know h by inferring it from (his knowledge of) b, then b is evidence for h for that inferrer. There is some doubt whether such an inference is psychologically possible since it is doubtful whether one could know b without also knowing that Jordan was male *simpliciter* (and *not* via inference from b), which is the real evidence for h since it is the real premise of a psychologically possible good inference. Sometimes, on the other hand, one can come to know something h by inferring it from a (known) consequence c of a (known) theory T. If one knows T but has not yet derived c from it, T is evidence for h for one on my psychological good inference conception of evidence; one can know h by inferring it from T via first inferring c.

Having given my alternative diagnoses of Achinstein's counterexamples to the positive relevance and high probability definitions of evidence, I want to mention some examples that he uses to motivate his own theory. I will briefly explain how these examples are supposed to do that and present Achinstein's (main) definition of evidence. I will not discuss his theory in any great detail. I will merely highlight one feature of it that is the final elaboration of an already very elaborate theory. The reason I do so, and the reason I discuss his positive motivating examples, is to make the case that a much less elaborate solution to Achinstein's counterexamples and a much less elaborate account of his examples is right under his nose: e is evidence for h for an inferrer just in case he could know h by inferring it from e. I will then close the chapter by discussing whether my psychological knowledge-based account of evidence can be expanded to a broader propositional knowledge-based account of evidence. I will suggest that it is unlikely, and that this is not much of a problem.

e: Arthur has a rash on his arm that itches.

b: Arthur was weeding yesterday bare-armed in an area filled with poison ivy, to which he is allergic.

h: Arthur's arm was in contact with poison ivy. (Achinstein 2001, 152)

Achinstein claims that *e* is evidence for *h*—it is "a good reason to believe *h*"—given the background *b*. On my psychological conception of inference, an inferrer who knows *b* can *ceteris paribus* know *h* by inferring it from *e*; *e* is evidence for *h* for such an inferrer.[31] Achinstein also claims (and I can agree) that *h* is a good reason to believe *e* given *b*, and, further, *e* is a good reason to believe *h* in the following case where neither proposition is intrinsically suited to be more *explanans* than *explanandum*:

e: Arthur has a rash on his right arm that itches.

b: Arthur was weeding yesterday using both hands with both arms bare in an area filled with poison ivy, to which he is allergic.

h: Arthur has a rash on his left arm that itches.

⋮

The general principle I am proposing is this:

General Principle: If, given *e* and *b*, the probability is high that there is an explanatory connection between *h* and *e*, then, given *e* and *b*, *e* is a good reason to believe *h*. (Achinstein 2001, 153)

Again, I have no problem endorsing the claim that *e* is evidence for *h* for one who knows *b* *ceteris paribus*. Such a person could indeed know *h* by inferring it from *e*. Achinstein builds a complex theory of evidence that uses the notion of an explanatory connection heavily both to avoid the counterexamples to the positive relevance and high probability definitions and to account for what is going on in the poison ivy examples and others. He takes there to be no less than four concepts of evidence, although two are much more important than the others: potential evidence and veridical evidence. I will ignore the other two. Veridical evidence, although one of four main concepts of evidence, itself comes in strong and weak variants; each is defined in terms of potential evidence. Veridical evidence is so-called because *e* is veridical evidence for *h* only if *h* is true. Achinstein thinks that the central concept of evidence that scientists use requires that the hypothesis be true, and he is most concerned with such a concept. I remain neutral on that claim. What I am most concerned to argue is that Achinstein's considerations in favor of his view in fact support a superior veridical conception of evidence, my own, according to which e is indeed only evidence for h if h is true. If e is evidence for h for an inferrer, then he can know h by inferring it from e; since knowledge entails truth, h must be true. I will not explore the details of Achinstein's definitions or how he arrives at them; I am concerned with what differentiates strong from weak veridical evidence, and why.

e is potential evidence that h, given b, only if

1. P(there is an explanatory connection between h and $e|e\&b) > \frac{1}{2}$
2. e and b are true
3. e does not entail h. (Achinstein 2001, 170)

(OK, I'll mention *one* detail briefly. Achinstein wants clause (3) because that one is wearing a blue suit (e) is not evidence that one is wearing a suit (h). This might be just a matter of pragmatics; it is not *too* odd to say that e is a good reason for believing h. More importantly, it is perhaps psychologically impossible to infer h from e; to believe e just *is* to believe h. So e could not be the premise of an inference to h in the psychological sense of 'inference', good or bad. So it is not evidence for h.)

e is veridical evidence that h, given b, if and only if

1. e is potential evidence that h, given b
2. h is true
(3. There is an explanatory connection between e's being true and h's being true.) (Achinstein 2001, 174)

The parenthesized third condition is the difference between strong and weak veridical evidence. On my view of evidence, e and h are both true since they are known and knowable respectively, and b is covered by the psychological conception of good inference, as already explained. Achinstein resists the requirement that e, h, and b be known rather than true because he favors a propositional conception of evidence according to which e might be evidence for h even if no one is aware of that fact. (The prospects of a propositional conception of evidence more expansive than my own will be discussed below.) So, the differences between my notion of evidence and Achinstein's strong veridical evidence appear to be the nonpropositional nature of my notion, the presence of knowledge as fundamental in my definition, and the absence of explanatory connection as fundamental in my definition. Actually, it is not, I suggest, as clear as that. Why does Achinstein

feel he needs a strong notion of veridical evidence that adds the third condition?

> The strong concept is relevant for certain "Gettier cases" purporting to show that justified true belief is not sufficient for knowledge. Suppose I am justified in believing (*h*) this coin will land heads on the 1001st toss, since I know that (*e*) it has landed heads each time on the first 1000 tosses, and (*b*) that it has a strong physical bias towards heads; but I have no way of knowing that an extremely unlikely external force, not its physical bias, will cause it to land heads on the 1001st toss. The usual view is that under these circumstances, although I have a justified true belief that *h*, I do not know that *h* is true. Requiring that my justification contain veridical evidence in the strong sense precludes this sort of case. (Achinstein 2001, section 8.4, note 2, 174)

To exclude Gettier cases from the domain of hypotheses for which *e* is evidence is not quite to say that *e* is evidence for *h* only if knowledge of *e* enables one to know *h*.[32] Excluding Gettier cases excludes unknown unknown (allegedly) justified yet true beliefs from what *e* is evidence for. *e* can still be evidence for known unknown hypotheses *if they are true* on Achinstein's definition of veridical evidence (strong or weak). Let us recall John and Bill from the first lottery counterexample. Recall that *e* is: On Tuesday, all the lottery tickets except those of John and Bill were destroyed, and on Wednesday one of the remaining tickets was drawn at random. However, John still owns 100 times more tickets than Bill. Achinstein's gripe with the positive relevance definition is that it declares *e* evidence that *Bill* won; Achinstein says that, on the contrary, it is evidence that John won. Having defined veridical evidence several chapters later, is *e* still evidence that John won for Achinstein? Provided John actually does win. If John is unlucky and Bill wins, then it is not true that John won, which is a necessary condition for *e* to be veridical evidence that John won. If John does win, then there will be "an explanatory connection" between *e*'s being true and the hypothesis that John won's being true for Achinstein, and so we will have (strong) veridical evidence that John won. If John loses, *e* is only *potential* evidence that John won, a potential that fails, against the odds, to be fulfilled.

Whether *e* is evidence for John's winning—whether it is a good reason to believe that he did in the theoretically most central sense for Achinstein, that of veridical evidence—should not depend on whether John actually won. Achinstein wants to rule out Gettier cases, which leads to distinguish-ing cases where the very same evidence enables one to know a hypothesis and to gain an unknown unknown (allegedly) justified belief in the hypothesis; only the former cases illustrate strong veridical evidence for the hypothesis. Many philosophers will balk at that consequence both of Achinstein's central definition of evidence *and* my own. The cases are distinguished for him and for me because of the presence or absence of knowledge.

For Achinstein, *mere* truth provides a distinction between cases of genuine evidence and cases of suboptimal (mere potential) evidence. My definition of evidence, on the other hand, finds no distinction among such cases because there is no distinction in the facts about knowledge. One cannot know that John won whether he did or not on the basis of e; consequently, e is not evidence that John won. One can know that John very likely won on the basis of e *whether he did or not;* that claim is what e is evidence for. My definition of evidence, which dovetails very neatly with my knowledge-based account of justified belief (and hence "good reasons" for believing), is *less* (allegedly) objectionably externalist than Achinstein's since he accepts all my externalist distinctions and more besides. If we abandon his proprietary externalist distinctions, we end up with a *much* simpler account of evidence than Achinstein's—which is more or less explicitly knowledge-based in some respects anyway. Neither do we need his *other,* less central notions of evidence (potential evidence and so on); far better to note that there are various competing *false* views on the extension of the evidence-for relation, and leave it at that.[33]

4.6   A Propositional Knowledge–based Conception of Evidence?

Many philosophers want an evidence-for relation that holds between sets of propositions *regardless* of whether anyone knows or even entertains the propositions that occupy the evidence role in the relation. Achinstein is, as we have seen, a propositionalist, but he does require the evidence (and the background propositions) to be true,[34] and, in the case of veridical evidence, he requires that the hypothesis be true, too. Many philosophers will want to go further, hoping for an evidence relation that can hold between false evidence propositions and hypotheses for which the evidence is evidence. For true propositions, such an expansive relation might coincide in extension with Achinstein's definition, and, for known propositions, it might coincide with my own.

If my knowledge-based good inference definition of evidence is correct, a more expansive propositional definition might be more desirable to some than my psychological definition that requires that evidence be the actual knowledge of a particular individual. Since no one holds out hope any more that we can develop an inductive logic possessing even remotely the same rigor and precision as deductive logic, it is questionable whether *formalizing* inductive inference and evidence relations is of any worth. If *that* is questionable, an expansive propositional definition of evidence has no obvious advantage over a narrower psychological definition, I suggest. Nevertheless, let us explore the prospects of an expansive propositional definition that is broadly consistent with our conclusions up to this point.

A propositionalist will want to follow Achinstein and numerous others in making the background knowledge of an inferrer an explicit relatum in the evidence relation. That is, he will wish to talk in terms similar to Achinstein's of e's being evidence for h *given* b; evidence-for is a three-place relation for the propositionalist. The background knowledge cannot be left implicit in the particular inferrer who could come to know the hypothesis through inference from the evidence as it is on my psychological conception of evidence since the propositionalist wants a definition that extends to evidence relations on which no one is in a position actually to base an inference. To *have* b as one's background knowledge it will not be enough to know the propositions in b. There will be situations in which e is evidence for h (given b) for S_1 who knows b but not for S_2 who knows b because S_1, but not S_2, can come to know h through inference from e on account of S_2 *also* knowing something that is a defeater for knowledge of h.[35] b represents *total* background knowledge bearing on the inference from e to h. For e to be *your* evidence that h given b, b has to be the only (relevant?) set of the propositions that you know (apart from e itself).[36]

So, the idea behind the more expansive propositional but still knowledge-based definition of evidence is to get knowledge out of the definition itself. e is evidence for h given b regardless of whether anyone believes e or has b as their total (relevant) background knowledge. To *have* that evidence, for it to be *your* evidence, it is necessary and sufficient for you to know e and have b as your total relevant background knowledge. Further, it is sufficient for you to know h if you are in that situation that you infer it from e.

But we will need more relata than e, b, and h, however, if the propositionalist definition is to coincide with the psychological definition with respect to evidence that is actually known, because of Gettier cases.[37] The difference between one who knows that h and a Gettierized counterpart who has an (allegedly) justified, true belief that h is *not* a difference in background knowledge. On the contrary, it is bad luck in the Gettier victim's *external* environment that leads to his failure to know that h. With better luck, he would have known that h by inferring it from his belief that e, possessing exactly the same background knowledge of the propositions in b. So, we will need an anti-Gettier relatum. I hesitate to speculate what that might be. The environmental factors that can Gettierize a would-be knower are very numerous; do we want as a fourth relatum a set of propositions g that includes negations of all of the propositions whose truth would Gettierize someone who knew e and had b as their total relevant background knowledge were they to infer h? Which propositions are members of g is likely to be very different depending upon the nature of the propositions that form e, h, and b. Should we include a complete history of a possible current state of the world in g to guarantee that we have *at least* the right propositions in g to bar Gettierization?

The *current* state of the world will likely not be enough, however. Whether someone who knows e and b can know h by inferring it from e might very well depend upon the *history* of the individual and/or his environment. Perhaps whether a *faculty* delivers knowledge depends upon its function in something like the way Plantinga (1993a) demands, and its function depends upon its history for evolutionary (or design) reasons.[38] Whether someone could know h by inference might also depend on *modal* facts about, for example, what he would have believed in similar circumstances, and on whether his inferential processes are in general reliable.[39] I take it that those modal facts will supervene on nonmodal facts that are hence all that would need to be included in g, but not on the nonmodal facts that obtain at a single time. Historical facts will have to be included in g, and which historical facts will depend heavily on e and b and h; perhaps g will have to specify an entire world history if we are to ensure that we capture all the facts needed to prevent Gettierization in every case.[40]

The fourth relatum is likely to be so unmanageably complex as to be of no philosophical utility whatsoever—all we will be able to do is gesture in its direction. Such a ghostly presence will not add any *greater* rigor and precision to the propositional definition of evidence than was present in the narrower psychological definition. Once again, by having "knowledge first" *and* last, we achieve far more precision than views that seek to replace knowledge as a foundational notion in epistemology. Evidence is best seen as a relation between what *is* known and what *can* be known in practice on that basis through inference, not as a relation between propositions that might be interpreted more or less strongly in terms of what can be known in principle and what can also be known in principle on that basis.

To close this chapter and the book, let us consider one last time my nemesis, the proponent of U-justification, and a suggestion that he might make. Forget knowledge, he might say. We should define the evidence-for relation in propositional terms with U-justification as the goal of those who actually possess evidence. If e is evidence for h given b, then one who knows (or, perhaps, is U-justified in believing) e and has b as his or her background knowledge (or background U-justified beliefs) can come to a U-justified belief in h by inferring it from e. Gettier cases are merely U-justified, true beliefs, so if we allow that the evidence-for relation holds between e, b, and h regardless of whether an inference from knowledge that e to h might produce a (true or false) merely U-justified belief in h, we can retain a simple three-place propositional evidence-for relation.

Or so my nemesis claims. But it is not so, quite apart from all the other problems with the notion of U-justification. For U-justification is, as I have stressed many times, an intuitive notion of would-be knowledge. One who has a merely U-justified belief (an unknown unknown belief) would have known were it not for exceptional bad luck in his external environment; in unexceptional circumstances, he would have known. But to even get into the position where you would have known but for bad luck requires having had a certain history, according to the considerations outlined above. Unless your faculties have the right history, they will have a much more deep-rooted problem that prevents them yielding knowledge than an exceptional case of bad luck. Something similar can be said for those many cases where counterfactual and reliabilist factors are needed for knowledge. The world needs to have had the right kind of history for the appropriate counterfactuals to be true of one (in, for example, the beliefs one would have formed) or to be using an in-general reliable process that will leave one at least U-justified when one suffers exceptional bad luck in one's external environment. Once again, we will need to add a fourth relatum g to our propositional definition of evidence-for to account for the kinds of historical fact that must obtain for someone to be U-justified in inferring h from e given background knowledge b. g is likely to depend heavily on e and h and is likely to resist general formulation unless g includes a large chunk of an entire world history. Perhaps a smaller chunk than the knowledge-based propositionalist will have to incorporate, but not smaller by enough to render U-justification-based propositionalism significantly more attractive. We see a final time how the utility of a notion of justification distinct from knowledge has been vastly overplayed in epistemology. We are better off without it. Knowledge first. And knowledge last.

Notes

Chapter 1

1. Shortly after I started using the terms 'known unknown' and 'unknown unknown' in the manner explained below, the U.S. Defense Secretary Donald Rumsfeld famously used those terms in a rather different manner—and certainly in a rather different context! As I use the terms, they are properties of *beliefs*. As Rumsfeld used them, they are properties of *propositions*, of that which is believed. There are things we know that we do not know—Rumsfeld's known unknown. There are things that we do not know but that we do not know that we do not know—we erroneously take ourselves to know them, Rumsfeld's unknown unknown.

2. We will address notions of *warrant* that depart from received wisdom in large part to avoid problems with Gettier cases in section 1.3.1.

3. Provided that minimal reflection on such matters does not trigger skeptical doubts in me, as it does not for most—even most philosophers.

4. I arguably would also lose such justification if I merely came to *believe,* even unjustifiably, that I did not know that I had a $10 bill even if I otherwise *would* have known—even if I am not a Gettier victim.

5. Linda Zagzebski (1996, 284) is one philosopher who does stress the bad luck involved in the Gettier cases.

6. The well-known fake barn example is attributed to Carl Ginet, although it came to prominence in Goldman 1976. Normally, forming a belief that there is a barn over there having looked at a barn in the middle distance is enough to know that there is a barn over there. However, if one is, unbeknownst to oneself, in an area containing far more facsimile barns constructed for a movie than real barns, one cannot know that there is a barn over there just by seeing a barn—a *real* barn—in the middle distance even if one's vision is working perfectly. One's true belief so formed is allegedly justified, however.

The Ford case derives from Gettier's original article (Gettier 1963). One has a lot of evidence that a particular colleague owns a Ford, and one forms the belief that one has *a* colleague who owns a Ford. In fact, the particular colleague to which one's evidence points just sold his car, and there is *another* colleague who owns a Ford, although one has no evidence that he does. One's true belief that one has a colleague who owns a Ford does not constitute knowledge, although it is (allegedly) justified.

For a discussion of what "good evidence" amounts to, see chapter 4.

7. I trust I do not need to define precisely what I mean by 'relevant mental state' here; what I am saying should be clear enough, and fairly uncontroversial. By 'relevant', I do not mean to imply 'all', in part because Williamson (2000) argues that knowledge itself is a mental state.

8. See Heller 1999 for one instance of this quite common claim.

9. Crispin Wright (1991) makes just such a suggestion; the oral expression of the sentiment is common.

10. There is perhaps a notion of justification that I call 'reasonableness' in that section that encompasses the unknown unknown beliefs as well as knowledge, but it is a notion that is parasitic upon knowledge, and it is not one of the important or central notions of justification in any case.

11. Although a true, known unknown belief is not a Gettier case, it is, of course, a counterexample to the definition of knowledge as justified, true belief *if* the known unknown beliefs are genuinely justified, just as a Gettier case—a true, *unknown* unknown belief—is such a counterexample if the unknown unknown beliefs are genuinely justified.

Of course, *I* think it is *true* that knowledge is justified, true belief, but that that truth does not support a traditional definition of knowledge.

12. We will return to "good reasons" and how to characterize them in our discussion of evidence in chapter 4.

13. If we assumed that probability is closed under conjunction, we could infer that probably (*p* and not-*p*), which is surely absurd. If the two claims 'probably *p*' and 'probably not-*p*' are implicitly relativized to different subjects, then, since there is no single subject (or group of subjects) for whom the proposition that (*p* and not-*p*) is probable, we cannot infer that probably (*p* and not-*p*) from the two original claims. But there are far worse (and well-known) problems with the assumption that probability is closed under conjunction than those introduced by ignoring the implicit relativization of probability to subjects. We will explore those problems in section 2.4.

14. There should be no problem for anything that I say if probabilistic belief content *and the believing of it* can be defined in concepts more psychologically primitive than that of probability—if sense can be made of the relevant notion of degrees of belief, for example—although I very much doubt that that can be done.

15. So it would seem, anyway; we will examine Plantinga's contrary view that he has been *somewhat* misinterpreted below.

16. Zagzebski and Merricks argue for this claim on similar grounds: any truth-independent notion of warrant used to define knowledge will render the definition open to Gettier-like counterexamples.

17. Even if there is such a thing as warrant, it is unclear *why* we should expect the notion of evaluative justification and the notion of warrant to apply to the very same beliefs.

18. I agree with Plantinga and others that the intuitiveness of more orthodox notions of justification arises in large part from a conflation of blamelessness and justification (about which I shall talk more in section 1.3.4). An account of errors that are at least as important in providing intuitive support for such notions will be the subject of section 2.3.

19. Plantinga only explicitly mentions Merricks not Zagzebski in the cited article.

20. Feldman (2000) no longer endorses the stronger claim, instead suggesting that if one adopts an attitude toward a proposition at all, it should be the attitude (and, he says, there is one and only one, understanding withholding belief and disbelief as attitudes) that one's evidence supports. One is not, on Feldman's later view, generally obligated on purely epistemic grounds to adopt an attitude toward a proposition.

21. I will posit a quite different motivation for internalism in section 2.3.

22. See section 1.3.4 for some discussion of an externalist response to the new evil-demon problem; some externalists do not acknowledge it as a genuine problem, and I will argue that this is the appropriate stance to take.

23. I will ignore this nicety in much of the following simply to avoid verbosity. It parallels the claim that the most central epistemic obligations by far are negative obligations, beliefs that one ought not have as opposed to beliefs that one ought to have.

24. At least if the claim is that belief aims at truth *simpliciter,* rather than something that at least *entails* truth.

25. Williamson (2000, ch. 1) makes just such a claim.

26. I expect some internalist dissent here. I discuss internalism at the end of this section and again at the end of the next chapter.

27. If there are several primary epistemic goals, then they might conflict in an individual case—one fulfills one goal by forming a given belief, but *not* forming the belief fulfills another. In such a case, it is conceivable that one ought not form the belief. What I am arguing is that if forming a belief satisfies one or many primary

epistemic goals, and not forming it does not satisfy any primary epistemic goal, then it is inconceivable that one nevertheless ought not form the belief.

28. His mental states differing only insofar as the change in external circumstances entails such a difference—as it would on Williamson's view mentioned in note 7.

29. One is tempted to say that no matter how well one knows one's own mind, there is almost no proposition about the external world that one is thereby guaranteed to know. But again, that characterization threatens to conflict with Williamson's views.

30. Kornblith makes these observations primarily to argue that voluntarism about belief is not entailed by the existence of epistemic obligations.

31. In chapter 4, I will suggest some exceptions to this general rule. Sometimes, one can infer justified beliefs—that is, beliefs that constitute knowledge—from unjustified beliefs.

32. "In fact, as is clear, the more active and faster a man is, the further astray he will go when he is running on the wrong road"—Francis Bacon, *Novum Organum*, trans. and ed. Urbach and Gibson 1.61, cited in Zagzebski 1996 (96). Alvin Goldman (1986, 102) makes a similar criticism of "epistemic decision theory," which is Bayesian in the relevant sense.

33. I owe thanks to Robert Howell and Mark Heller for bringing this point to my attention.

34. Although many properties that some beliefs have are objectively bad from the perspective of truth-conduciveness, making his nonfactualism only partial.

35. The best externalist response is perhaps to say that our goal is justification, which, when things go well, amounts to knowledge, knowledge itself being impossible as a goal since our goals are subject to *some* internalist constraints, and we cannot distinguish between knowledge and the unknown unknown from the inside. It does not follow from the fact that we aim at justification that we aim at the unknown unknown beliefs—that we aim at justification going *badly*. I simply contest the assumption that our goals are subject to internalist constraints strong enough to rule out knowledge as a goal. In section 1.3.2, I stressed that there is no need to demand an epistemic goal that can be achieved infallibly, and knowledge is an acceptable goal that can be *fallibly* aimed at.

36. Depending upon what one takes to be required for testimonial knowledge (see chapter 3), it might be suggested that the scientifically benighted society possesses unknown unknown, justified beliefs, which are arguably evaluatively justified, not merely blameless. Had their society not been scientifically benighted, the beliefs acquired therefrom would have constituted knowledge. It is bad luck in the external

environment—in this case, the rest of society—that prevents them from acquiring knowledge.

This stretches the concept of unknown unknown justification well beyond its intuitive bounds. It is intuitive to say that an unknown unknown belief *that p* is justified because the believer would have known *that p* had he not suffered from bad luck in his external environment *in this particular instance.* The scientifically benighted would have formed beliefs very different in content had he not been a member of the scientifically benighted society; as it is, his problems are not confined to exceptional cases of bad luck, but are quite general. All that is intuitive is that his beliefs are blameless in some sense.

37. Plantinga and other proponents of warrant make similar claims. A quite different explanation of the judgment will be given in section 2.3.

38. The Internet search engine Google shows that the majority of occurrences of the phrase 'justified belief' occur in online philosophical texts, or in texts that one would expect to be heavily influenced by philosophy, such as arguments against the existence of God. The exception is occurrences of the term in the law—not so much in academic study thereof, but in the text of laws themselves. Requiring the law-abiding (in many cases, the police) to have a "justified belief" that *p* can, it seems, be unproblematically interpreted as requiring them to know that *probably p* and so, in my terms, to have a justified belief that probably *p*. In section 2.3, we will revisit the usage of the phrase 'justified belief that *p*' to denote what is, strictly speaking, justified belief that probably *p*—and the confusion that this has produced when philosophers engage in it. (Lawmakers will emerge unscathed.)

This usage of 'justified belief' also, I suspect, reflects what nonphilosophers most often mean when they call a belief reasonable or not. The quasi-technical notion of reasonable belief defined below is secondary, if present at all, in colloquial talk.

39. Such a use of 'justification' brings up the related questions of what constitutes good reasons for believing a proposition, and what constitutes good evidence for a hypothesis. These questions will receive full answers in chapter 4.

40. In response to Bonjour's (1985) arguments against reliabilist theories of justification, one detail of many reliabilist theories is to require at least that a justified believer not believe that his belief was formed by an unreliable process or that it is probably false.

41. Bonjour's arguments against reliabilism, referred to in note 40, fit this mold.

42. Since (propositional) knowledge does not come in degrees, if one does identify justification and knowledge, one proceeds no further. I will have a little more to say on the matter in note 4 of the next chapter.

Further reasons for avoiding appeal to degrees of justification are provided in section 2.5.1.

Chapter 2

1. I discuss less important objections to the arguments in the course of presenting the arguments themselves.

2. "Warrant" is Williamson's term; Unger, and DeRose following him, say that one "represents oneself" as knowing that p in so asserting. Williamson's use of the term is not to be confused with Plantinga's technical notion, of course.

3. I am, of course, supposing that it is possible to gain justified beliefs and knowledge through testimony, an assumption that should need no defense nowadays.

4. Perhaps any theory of justification that allowed the recipient of testimony to have a more highly justified belief acquired solely on the basis of testimony than the testifier himself would be *ipso facto* objectionable. Perhaps not, however—the testifier is acting as a filter to make the trustworthiness of his assertions exceed that of his raw beliefs, and that is not obviously an absurd notion. For me, the notion of a belief being *more* justified than another justified belief is, strictly speaking, nonsense— knowledge does not come in degrees. I will discuss Jennifer Lackey's (1999) alleged counterexample to the claim that the testifiee cannot gain testimonial knowledge that p unless the testifier himself knows that p in section 3.4. (Even if one thought that Lackey's counterexample was genuine, we can stipulate that Andy and Bob's case is not relevantly similar to it.)

What *does* come in degrees is the probabilistic content of the proposition known. One who merely knows that it is quite likely that p can be said to be "less justified" in his belief "that p" than one who merely knows that it is extremely likely that p who is himself "less justified" in his belief "that p" than one who knows categorically that p. We will return to this perfectly serviceable way of not speaking strictly in section 2.3.

5. It is even possible that Bob knows that Andy does *not* know (Andy might tell him that he does not know, for example), but is merely justified (assuming such a thing is possible for the sake of argument, of course) if Andy's justified belief is a member of the known unknown class. (If it is a member of the unknown unknown class, just as Andy could not come to know that he did not know without also losing justification for his belief, Bob could not come to know that Andy was merely justified in believing that p and acquire justification for believing that p through knowing that about Andy.) Bob still ought to be able to acquire a justified, true belief on the basis of Andy's testimony.

6. I say that the goal is to transmit beliefs rather than justified beliefs. This does not entail that it is also a goal of assertion to transmit *false* or *unjustified* beliefs. I might have the goal of learning to play the piano without having the goal of learning to play the piano well. This is not to say that I also have as my goal to play the piano badly.

7. We suppose here that the notion of warrant can be applied univocally to both assertion and belief. If 'warrant' is *just* employed as a term for a component in the definition of knowledge that is not alleged to have any independent status (that is, it is not also a deontological or evaluative notion of justification), then my arguments do not touch it, nor are they intended to. I doubt knowledge can be defined in terms of such a notion, but arguing the case is not my concern right now—see section 2.5 for a discussion of the definition of knowledge.

8. If definite descriptions and possessive pronouns are also quantifiers, the actual truth communicated might be considerably more verbose, but I trust that the idea is clear.

9. I am not the first to propose that Williamson's knowledge rule governing assertion entails a corresponding knowledge rule governing belief. Crispin Wright (1996, 935) takes this line on the grounds that "the . . . notion of warranted assertion . . . is simply the exterior counterpart of warranted *belief*." (This sentence is taken from a single paragraph concerning the knowledge rule—he does not give any further argument, nor can he be expected to given the context in which his discussion occurs.) Wright, however, takes the entailment to be grounds for rejecting Williamson's knowledge rule governing assertion since "[the] long tradition in epistemology of distinguishing knowledge and reasonable belief may indeed be misguided; but, if it is, it will demand a very substantial argument to show it" (ibid.). I hope this book will provide such an argument. (Wright also notes that assertions made in many contexts seem to fall short of expressing knowledge, contexts such as "medical diagnosis, weather forecasting, ordinary psychology, history, economics [and] plant ecology," and he seems to think that a presumption of warranted assertion in those contexts outweighs the intuition that Williamson's lottery assertions are unwarranted. I suggest that ordinary politics and ordinary journalism should be added to Wright's list.)

10. Actually, she presents the paradoxes as concerning knowledge on the one hand and *rationality* on the other. However, it is clear that the rationality paradox can be restated without loss in terms of justification, and footnote 13 of Nelkin's paper indicates that she is happy with such a restatement provided that justification is not understood as warrant in Plantinga's sense. I will briefly mention how a proponent of justification as warrant might approach the paradoxes below.

11. Nelkin's locution "It is rational for Jim to believe" does not entail that Jim actually believes, and I am keeping this feature of the argument intact in my representation of it in terms of justification. I intend to be expressing the thought that if Jim does not believe that his ticket will lose, then if he were to do so, his belief would be justified, and if he does so believe, then his belief is justified.

12. However, as we will see in section 2.4, there is a *third* version of the paradox that, if one speaks loosely, can be expressed in the very same terms as the justification paradox above, although, strictly speaking, it is a quite distinct paradox and should

be likewise expressed. Denying what is, loosely speaking, a conjunction rule for justification is *unquestionably* the solution to the third version of the lottery paradox— although, strictly speaking, the solution denies no such thing.

13. There might well be reasons for denying that knowledge is closed under conjunction in cases presented indirectly by lotteries. Matthew Weiner (2004) provides such cases, building on Hawthorne 2004. He supposes that all of one's friends have lottery tickets and we stipulate that only one ticket is possessed by a nonfriend and that nonfriend wins the lottery. One arguably knows of each friend that he will never be rich (if we make appropriate assumptions about one's friends' financial acumen), but one does not know that all of one's friends will never be rich (although that is true in the imagined circumstances), which claims can easily be restated as a giant conjunction that is not known despite knowledge of each conjunct.

14. If we employ a deontological paraphrase, to say that it is permissible for Jim to believe that his ticket will lose is to say that if he were to so believe, then he would know. His belief would be in accord with the epistemic duty to believe only if one knows.

15. She reviews and finds wanting a number of alternative actual and potential joint diagnoses of the two versions of the paradox (although not my own).

16. 'Rational' being the term that she employs, as previously noted. Obviously, this condition on justified belief is not supposed to form part of a definition of justification because of any such definition's obvious circularity.

17. Although perhaps she means to assert this of the explicitly probabilistic examples alone, theoretical beliefs arising from inferences to the best explanation that fail to constitute knowledge having sufficient explanatory connection to their objects to be justified. Her text is unclear on the point since her example of a general belief justified by (a disposition to) justified belief in explanatory connections that are not causal is the belief that all objects on Earth are affected by its gravitational pull. This, of course, is something that we know and so is not a member of the known unknown class of allegedly justified beliefs. It remains the case, then, that the examples that she provides of causal and explanatory connections (potential) belief in which is supposed to be essential to justification are precisely those connections that are necessary for knowledge in the relevant cases. She gives no indication that she would accept weaker connections than that; if she did, it would not *ipso facto* supply her rejection of (1*) with a genuine explanation of its falsity in any case.

18. Here is what Plantinga (1993a, 166) has to say about why properly functioning faculties with the right design plan would not produce such beliefs:

[some] components of the basic account of warrant must be *generalized* to apply properly to the case of probability. We must say, here, that the design plan is successfully aimed at an appropriate correlation between the objective conditional probability of

a proposition A on a proposition B, and the degree of confidence invested by [the believer] in A on the basis of B. A good or successful design plan . . . will be one such that there is a substantial statistical probability that a propositional attitude formed in accordance with [it] . . . toward a proposition A, on the basis of a proposition B, will match or approximate the objective probability of A on B.

As stated in section 1.2.2, I think that degree of confidence in the relevant sense has to be cashed out in terms of the probabilistic content of degreeless beliefs. Given that, a design plan aimed at yielding *knowledge,* and a faculty that functions properly in accord with it, will satisfy Plantinga's constraints, broadly speaking, irrespective of the issue of warrant. One will believe that p is probable to such-and-such a degree only if p really is that probable for one.

19. One might object that categorical belief that one will lose is entirely appropriate, but the *degree* of that belief should be less than maximal. If talk about degrees of belief is interpreted in terms of simple belief in explicitly (which is not to say *precise*) probabilistic propositions, as I suggested in section 1.2.2, the "objection" to my view is no objection at all—it is my view.

Hawthorne (2004) stresses that if the expected value of one's lottery ticket (the product of its chance of winning and the value of the prize) is, say, two cents, then it is irrational to sell it for a penny. If one were to sell it for a penny, one would be acting as if one knew that one was going to lose (or that its expected value was less than it is—I will ignore this qualification); since one does not, one's action would be irrationally overconfident. In at least many cases, the limits of rational action are the limits of knowledge.

20. An important contribution to the irrationality of his epistemic situation is made by the fact that he has *considered* the proposition that he has clean hands.

21. Defining just which situations can be properly ignored in full generality for all possible knowledge is almost certainly at least as difficult as defining knowledge itself; I will not attempt it.

22. Some such pusillanimists arguably produce counterexamples to the KK principle which states that if one knows that p, then one knows that one knows that p. The much-discussed test subject who hesitantly gives the correct answer "p" to the question to which that is the correct answer is such a pusillanimist if we fill in the details in the right way. The test subject knows that p, but does not believe (and hence does not know) that he knows that p; some such subjects *can* know that they know that p, but irrational hesitancy leads them not to believe that they know. If only they were to believe that they knew that p, they would know that they knew that p. Other such subjects are perhaps so lacking in confidence that their belief that p itself would be abandoned at the slightest provocation; it is arguable that they do not even know that p.

23. A more than cursory investigation of the links between rational action and rational belief construed as knowledge would take another book, so I will leave the matter here.

24. If the principle is restricted to beliefs that would be true if formed, the argument to follow will still proceed.

25. And, *ex hypothesi,* a true belief on the matter would have had beneficial consequences. I stipulate this since I do not wish to assume that a true belief itself is a good even if it has neutral or even harmful consequences. If a true belief *does* have beneficial consequences, one should, in some sense, form it *in addition* to the fact that one should experience those consequences (quite apart from the fact that they are consequences of a true belief).

26. I emphasize once again that one's obligations and subsequent blameworthiness are generated by a combination of epistemic considerations *and* prudential and other nonepistemic considerations particular to one's situation. One is not in general obligated to know what one *could* know, and neither, as we stressed in section 1.3.4, does blameworthiness follow from unmet obligation in all or most cases. In some cases these phenomena go together, and we can suppose that the proposed situation is one of these cases.

27. The optimal defense of the RBK account endorses just such a possibility, as I explain immediately below.

28. If one interprets the 'R' of the RBK rule along the lines of the 'J' in the J rule, the RBK rule is arguably *stronger* than the knowledge rule itself. A justified belief that one knows that *p* will, in unexceptional circumstances where one is not subject to bad luck in one's external environment, constitute knowledge that one knows that *p*. Such an RBK rule is not as strong as a KK rule that *requires* one to know that one knows what one asserts, but, in unexceptional circumstances, asserters who follow an RBK rule thus interpreted will know that they know what they assert.

29. Of course, *belief* is still a component of the J rule, just not belief that one knows; it is no less a component of the knowledge rule in any important sense since knowledge entails belief.

30. An account of *warrant* (in the sense of section 1.3.1) will not meet the burden of proof since such an account, if successful, *avoids* the Gettier problem by classifying U-justified true beliefs as nevertheless unwarranted. There is no reason to think a successful definition of warrant will provide a basis for a successful nondisjunctive definition of U-justification.

31. Such utterances would be examples of the kind of exception to the knowledge rule governing assertion noted at the end of section 2.1.1. They would be cases where it is appropriate to assert a proposition—that one believes that *p*—although one does not know it since it is not true that one believes that *p*. However, another view is

that the belief sentence that one utters *is* true rather than being a falsehood used to communicate a truth. It is just that utterances of sentences apparently concerning belief in one proposition are sometimes made true by belief in a different but related proposition. It is not necessary to decide between these (and other) options in the philosophy of language for our purposes.

32. One mistakes the loose usage of 'belief' for the *only* usage of the term if one, so to speak, takes probability to reside in the attitude of belief itself rather than the proposition believed by endorsing one conception of "degrees of belief." One takes oneself to believe the proposition that the post office is a mile to the right in the situation described above, but to a fairly small *degree,* and one takes what is in fact simply belief that it is a mile to the right, strictly speaking, to be belief in the same proposition to a much higher degree. This is perhaps a way of preserving the literal truth of quotidian belief ascriptions, but not the only way, as we saw in the previous note. Some of the unfortunate consequences of taking the loose usage of 'belief' to be the only usage are explained immediately below.

33. See chapter 1, note 38.

34. Internalists are, however, far from the only epistemologists to indulge in such talk.

35. The influence a similar conflation has had on the literature concerning evidence will be the subject of a large part of chapter 4.

36. Of course, I have my own problems with reliabilism insofar as it does not identify justification and knowledge.

37. If the two believers are members of the same possible world, at least, and any relevant temporality is a component of the proposition believed—one can know at noon that it is raining and know at midnight that it is not raining, but what one knows at noon and midnight is not a proposition and that very proposition's negation.

38. It is, of course, often misleading to say merely that S believes that probably p if one knows that S has a categorical belief that p, for standard Gricean reasons. But it is not always inappropriate to so speak (and perhaps to mislead as a result), particularly if S is oneself, as guarded assertions show. My boss might well *know* that I will get a raise this year, but, upon questioning, merely says that I will probably get a raise. He thereby expresses something that he believes, and indeed knows—his assertion does not violate Williamson's knowledge rule.

39. As noted in section 2.3, 'say' cannot be used loosely just as 'know' cannot. If I say that there are probably mice in the basement, I cannot be truly described simply as having said that there were mice in the basement on that basis. That 'say' (and 'assert') and 'know' behave similarly is very consonant with Williamson's knowledge rule for assertion. If 'say' (and 'assert') could be used loosely, then we could not determine from correct reports of others' assertions (which is how 'say' is used much of the

time) whether the assertions reported upon were themselves correct *even if we knew all relevant facts about what the speaker did and did not know*. If Pyrrhus merely knew that he would probably achieve a swift victory, it makes a big difference whether he said without qualification that he would do so, or whether he merely said that he would probably do so. If Pyrrhus said the former, then he can be held to account for an incorrect assertion. If he said the latter, and one speaks loosely by reporting that he said that he would achieve a swift victory, one can oneself be held to account (by Pyrrhus, for example) since such loose speaking is always incorrect, and, indeed, false—what one said entails that Pyrrhus said something stronger than he actually said. (I am grateful to Daniel McLean for suggesting this example.)

That 'know' can only be used strictly is also very consonant with Williamson's view, which is also my own, that it is *knowledge* that is the fundamental epistemic notion in terms of which almost all others are to be explicated. The absence of the relevant loose usage of 'know', and the presence of such uses for 'belief' (and hence 'justified belief'), is, I suggest, a reflection of the objective epistemic order. That the language endorses only the strict usage for what is most fundamental is to be expected if it is to enable us *ever* to speak strictly on epistemic matters. (Those who hope to achieve epistemic clarity about what is most fundamental through technical notions and theories such as those of possible worlds, relevant alternatives, deontic logic, decision theory, and what have you will, of course, strongly disagree.)

40. Of course, the claim that there are justified beliefs that do not constitute knowledge is the *most* extreme example.

41. Hunter (1996) and Foley (1992), for example.

42. And such a meticulous author might express this belief that there are errors in his book in the preface, rendering his book as a whole inconsistent—not every statement could be true since if all the statements in the body of the text were true, the expression of fallibility in the preface would be false. Hence the name of the paradox.

43. One might object that commonsense concepts have often been successfully replaced or refined by technical counterparts: think of the Newtonian physicist's distinction between mass and weight superseding a commonsense conflation of the two notions. Such a comparison, I suggest, adds to the hubris of philosophical lack of respect for commonsense concepts.

44. Further details on how the commonsense theory of the mind is supposed to define implicitly the various commonsense mental states can be found in Lewis 1970, among other places.

45. David Armstrong (1968) is perhaps an exception.

46. For more on the notion of evidence, see chapter 4.

47. Such promiscuity is largely confined to chapter 3.

48. The stipulation that the same proposition and thinker are specified on both occasions is crucial. Everyone accepts that 'Bill knows that possums are nocturnal' can be false on one occasion and not on another because one is talking about different people both named 'Bill' on the two occasions. It is *commonly,* although far from universally, accepted that 'The ancient astronomers knew that Hesperus appeared in the morning sky' can be false as uttered in one context and true in another because 'that Hesperus appeared in the morning sky' picks out a different proposition in each context; a proposition only believed by someone who thinks of Hesperus *as called 'Hesperus'* in one context and a proposition about the planet Venus however one thinks of it in another. (Roughly speaking—the issues here are complicated.) Neither of these phenomena amount to contextualism about knowledge.

49. References to *not-p* will be largely implicit henceforth.

50. Which is not to say that there are not problems with even *formulating* such standards in an acceptable manner. Whatever it is, more or less of which is supposed to be required to be truly described as 'knowing', depending upon the context in which knowledge is ascribed, it had better not be something that we can understand only in terms of *knowledge* itself on pain of vicious circularity. The contention that what varies from context to context is how many "relevant alternatives" one must rule out—possible situations in which one's belief that p is false—in order to be said to know that p is problematic if we understand only what it is for an alternative to be relevant precisely because it is one that prevents knowledge unless it is known not to obtain. In chapter 4, I will argue that our grasp of the notion of evidence depends upon the concept of knowledge, and so we cannot formulate contextualism about knowledge by appeal to contextually varying standards of evidence. It almost goes without saying at this point that the invocation of contextually varying standards of "justification" is also unhelpful.

51. In chapter 3, we will briefly return to the matter of the case *for* contextualism in exploring the *real* moral of DeRose's Bank Cases (DeRose 1992).

Chapter 3

1. However, many of the arguments in the chapter proceed without relying upon the claim that justified belief simply is knowledge, and so I will often talk as though there are justified beliefs that do not constitute knowledge with occasional reminders of my official position that there are no such beliefs.

2. The KK view is only superficially similar to the KK principle that one knows that p only if one knows that one knows that p.

3. Some will say that we already had such a term—'justified' itself. Of course, I disagree, but it is useful to have a term that has the specified extension by stipulation.

4. For an explicit endorsement of a BK view—in particular, the simplest view that all it takes for a testifiee to derive knowledge that p from testimony that p provided by a testifier who knows that p is that the testifiee believe that p on the basis of that testimony, see Welbourne 1979, 1994.

5. A right that, as we will see, Fricker denies.

6. On the other hand, the statement "I trust what you say. And I do so because I know that you know what you are talking about" does not strike me as particularly deviant.

7. Burge explicitly endorses the comparison of testimony to memory, but not because of a conception of memory that is flawed in the above sense. Memory and testimony are both instances of what Burge calls "content preservation," where 'content' for Burge denotes something like information in one sense of the term, something dynamic that can be passed around rather than the proposition believed, remembered, or known, which is, I suppose, trivially preserved if the testifier that p and the testifiee both believe that p. (I do not pretend fully to understand what Burge means by 'content'.) Just as memory is the retrieval (not creation) of content *and its status as justified*, testimony is the transferral (not creation) of content and its justification to another party. On the JBK and KK views and the associated answers to the first question, which we will describe below, this figurative description of testimony is arguably inapt since the testifiee makes his own contribution to the justification of his testimonial belief. Its status as justified is not passively received from the testifier.

8. A known unknown (allegedly) justified belief in a proposition p that one has as a result of a perceptual experience is grounded in knowledge that probably p that one has as a result of that experience, which knowledge is inferred rather than derived from the experience in the relevant sense.

9. The default justification view is not interesting unless it claims that the justification that testimonial beliefs have by default is derived from testimony. The claim that beliefs formed as a result of testimony are in general justified for reasons independent of the fact that they were so formed is not a philosophical claim, but an empirical one, and a false claim at that.

10. I suppose that we could also define a term 'KU-justified' whose extension is the union of knowledge, the unknown unknown, justified beliefs, and the known unknown, justified beliefs. The claim that beliefs are KU-justified by default has so little initial appeal that I will only discuss it cursorily. If one has a testimonial belief that does not constitute knowledge, it would in *some* cases be K-justified and in other cases U-justified on the envisaged view. I have no idea what would determine into which category such a testimonial belief fell.

11. I am also not entirely sure that the position is coherent enough that the suppositions that I make for the sake of argument are as coherent as I will assume them to be for the sake of argument.

12. I will discuss Jennifer Lackey's (1999) alleged counterexample to this claim in section 3.4.

13. There are many interesting philosophical questions that arise from the evaluation and integration of distinct sources of (possibly conflicting) testimony, such as historians engage in. Some of those questions might well concern the evaluation of testimonial evidence in particular as opposed to the evaluation of evidence in general. However, these are not questions about testimonial knowledge in our sense since they do not concern the transfer of knowledge from testifier to testifiee.

14. An unfortunate ambiguity has arisen involving the term 'implicit belief' (and 'tacit belief', which is often used to mean the same thing[s]) in philosophy and related fields. It is often used to mean belief that is explicitly represented in the mind but inaccessible to consciousness; this is the sense in which our knowledge of grammar might be called 'implicit' or 'tacit'. This is not the sense of the term that I am using; I mean a belief that may very well be accessible to consciousness but that is not explicitly represented in the mind. The relation between the two senses is an open question. For an interesting development of the claim that the two senses are related, see Crimmins 1992. For more on implicit belief in my sense of that term, see also Field 1978 and Lycant 1986.

15. Which is not to say that it is uncontroversial that there are implicit beliefs; see Richard 1990 and Audi 1982 for argument that there are no such beliefs. I will not address those arguments here since it will not materially affect the discussion if the BK view is taken merely to involve a commitment to a testifiee having the kind of disposition to believe that the testifier knows that proponents of implicit belief take to constitute or at least correlate with an implicit belief that the testifier knows, whether or not they are right to do so.

16. It is not essential to the point that the assertion is made in the first person. If I assert that x is a better philosopher than y, where I am neither x nor y, it is not significantly easier for the uninformed to know what I testify to even if I know what I testify to. Neither is it necessary that someone else make a contrary assertion that y is a better philosopher than x, although that will make it even harder for the uninformed to become informed enough to know or be justified in believing what I testify to.

17. I do not mean to deny that it is logically and even nomologically possible that one subject a youth to a rigorous reeducation program and thereby give him enough beliefs and other propositional attitudes of an appropriate sort that he, in all important respects, has the mind of a middle-aged individual and so is capable of gaining (relatively easily) by testimony the kind of knowledge that a middle-aged individual but not a normal youth has or can gain (relatively easily) by testimony. It remains the case there is some knowledge that it is practically impossible for the middle-aged to give the young through testimony.

18. A further problem for the BK view (but not for the default justification view) arises with such testifiers whose reputation is not known to the testifiee. That a testifier is

regarded as a habitual liar means that one cannot know what he testifies to just by believing what he says even if in a particular case he does know what he testifies to. This is so whether or not the testifiee is aware of the testifier's reputation. His reputation (even if undeserved) functions as a social defeater for knowledge in the way that Harman's fabricated newspaper reports do (to be discussed further below), whether one has read them or not (Harman 1973). The testifier's reputation, it seems, can constitute a "stronger reason" to doubt his testimony than to accept it only if the testifiee is aware of that reputation. At least, we should demand a substantial explanation of what is meant by 'reason' if this is not so and the BK view is to amount to anything sufficiently determinate to discuss.

19. No one will contend that one is justified in believing testimony that *p* if and only if one is justified in believing that the testifier is *merely* justified in believing that *p*; that is, if one justifiably believes that the testifier does not know that *p*. In such a case, one is not justified in believing that *p* on the basis of the testifier's testimony that *p* by anyone's lights. Hence the appearance of the word 'know' even in the principle that concerns justified testimonial belief rather than testimonial knowledge. To believe justifiably that the testifier justifiably believes that *p* is to believe justifiably that the testifier knows that *p*.

U-justification is the sense of justification at play here for reasons discussed previously. If you have a known unknown, justified belief that *p* as a result of testimony that *p*, you know that *probably p* as a result of the testimony, but that knowledge and subsequent (alleged) justification is not derived from the testimony in the relevant sense.

20. Suppose that I have a merely (allegedly) justified belief that the testifier knows in the known unknown sense of 'justified'. That is, I know that the testifier *probably* knows that *p*, but not that he does. As previously stated, it is hard to see how I could know anything more than that *probably p*. Continuing the line of thought explored in the transmission discussion above, since one should only assert what one knows, I will be irresponsible if I tell another that *p* (rather than that probably *p*). A testifiee would be in a position, all other things being equal, to know that probably *p* from my testimony that probably *p*; but he cannot *derive* even knowledge that probably *p* from my categorical testimony that *p*. If he does not entirely trust me (that is, believe that *p* on my say-so), and the world and his background knowledge are appropriate, he might gain knowledge that probably *p* from knowledge that I said that *p*, but that knowledge would be inferential and not derived in the relevant sense from my testimony.

21. For an endorsement of its sufficiency, see Hardwig 1991, 1985.

22. I am not sure whether Graham would endorse the general line of thought.

23. In fairness to Graham, he says that the KK view is arguably too demanding if one has to know that the testifier knows "in an independent way"—independent of the testimony itself, that is. It is quite possible, then, that Graham is criticizing a

form of the KK view that no one has endorsed or ever would endorse unless he was comfortable with philosophical skepticism.

24. Perhaps neither characteristic of testimony is sufficient in general for knowledge without the presence of the other.

25. "For these reasons the Teaching Authority of the Church does not forbid that, in conformity with the present state of human sciences and sacred theology, research and discussions, on the part of men experienced in both fields, take place with regard to the doctrine of evolution, in as far as it inquires into the origin of the human body as coming from pre-existent and living matter—for the Catholic faith obliges us to hold that souls are immediately created by God." —Pius XII, *Humani Generis* 36 (initial part). Whatever qualities one inherits from one's parents, one can inherit in the standard fashion from prehuman ancestors as far as the Church is concerned. What one cannot inherit from those ancestors, one does not inherit from one's parents either: one's soul is immediately created by God.

26. Well, it is at least obvious that our knowledge of what words mean arises largely from others talking in our presence (and often to us). Saying that we thereby derive testimonial *beliefs* about what words mean (as opposed to, in the first instance, abilities, which might be what 'knowing what a word means' amounts to in at least some contexts) let alone testimonial (propositional) knowledge is far from unproblematic, but I will not explore the issue further, partially because it is an empirical one, and also because it would be peripheral to the rest of our discussion.

27. This is an empirical, not a philosophical, claim, and if you do not already know it, I cannot help you come to do so in the space of this chapter—not unless the BK view is true of testimony in general, at least.

Chapter 4

1. A vague claim, but one that I intend to be stronger than, for example, the claim that the conditional probability of the conclusion on the premises is high. How I explicate the notion of premises making a conclusion likely to be true will become clear below; it is a matter of one being able to know that the conclusion is likely to be true through inference from knowledge of the premises.

2. Despite the psychological foundation of my notion of inference, the propositional nature of the premises and conclusion makes talk of the *form* of an inference perfectly sensible, and I will engage in such talk below.

3. Actually, I will suggest below a very qualified positive answer to this question in exceptional cases. Even in those cases, the inference is partially but not entirely good.

4. Feldman's example (Feldman 1994, 177) of a defeated argument concerns someone whose premises are that a particular individual is a basketball player and that most basketball players are tall; the defeated argument has the conclusion that this

basketball player is tall. It is defeated for the individual because he believes (justifiably) that this basketball player is giving a talk on how he made it in the NBA even though he was short. On my view, the inference whose conclusion is that this basketball player is tall is no good even without the defeating background belief about the topic of the player's talk—there is extensive discussion of this matter below. All he can know on the basis of his statistical knowledge is that the player is *probably* tall or something similar, so that is the limit of good inference here. If he also has the defeating background belief, then he will not know that the player is even probably tall, of course.

5. We do not need to consider the metaphysical question of whether it is essential to inferences in the psychological sense that they occur in a particular psychological context. We are interested in giving an account of when an inference is *actually* good; we are not interested in whether a good inference is essentially good, or in whether it would be good were such-and-such counterfactual conditions to obtain.

6. As I argued in section 2.4, common reasons given for denying that justification is closed under conjunction are unpersuasive even if one does not identify justification and knowledge.

7. My definition of good inference will be similarly unhelpful in addressing other "paradoxes of confirmation" such as Hempel's paradox of the ravens (Hempel 1945), although they do not present problems for it. There is something unilluminating, although true, to say in such cases just as there is for the new riddle of induction.

8. See van Fraassen 1989 for a negative answer.

9. Giving an account of what the semantic deductive consequences of a proposition are and how one can in general determine them is the hardest part of filling in the sketch, of course.

10. One who knows that Newtonian mechanics is false can also know how the physical world will behave in many respects on the basis of Newtonian mechanics, although he does not do so by drawing inferences from Newtonian mechanics in the same sense as one who believes it. Rather, he will draw inferences from his knowledge that Newtonian mechanics is practically reliable although strictly speaking false.

11. Just how many bad inferences there are that nevertheless yield known conclusions is an interesting question, although not, perhaps, a strictly philosophical question. *Anyone* who is not the crudest of relativists believes that many religious beliefs are unjustified. Nevertheless, the Santa Claus and Newtonian examples suggest that such beliefs might nevertheless enable their adherents to gain knowledge through inference (moral knowledge, for example), and perhaps even knowledge that they might not otherwise gain. The adherents might be better off when judged by the standard of how much knowledge they possess than they would be if they did not hold such beliefs despite the fact that those beliefs are unjustified. Someone who did

not hold the unjustified beliefs in question might even utilize them to gain knowledge in the manner that one who knows Newtonian mechanics to be false can use it to gain knowledge of how the physical world will behave, *if* he knew them to be practically reliable for obtaining moral knowledge, for example. That, of course, is a rather big 'if'.

12. The term 'closure' is a little unfortunate since relatively few philosophers have claimed that one knows that *q* "automatically" if one knows the premises of a *modus ponens* inference. One has to make the connection through drawing an inference (Vogel 1990). In many cases, that inference is perhaps *implicit* in a sense similar to that employed in the previous chapter; it is not consciously entertained.

13. The classic discussion here is Nozick 1981.

14. Simplifying greatly, the reason for the failure of closure in Nozick's theory is that if we were brains in vats, we would still believe that we were not. If we had no hands, we would not believe that we did since if we had no hands that fact would obtain for a reason much more mundane than our being a brain-in-a-vat, and would be observable. This is why we know that we have hands, but not that we are not brains in vats for Nozick.

15. If there are even a great number of such unknown consequences for almost all cases of contingent knowledge, it is not promising to suppose that I do not *really* know where my car is parked but rather that it is parked on Not Utterly Safe St. unless it has been stolen, or impounded, or what have you. It would be hard to ascribe determinate content to my beliefs that really constitute knowledge, and even harder to suppose that we form such beliefs in the first place, or even could do so in practice. Not to mention that a similar proliferation of exceptions would have to be attached to each of the "first level" of exceptions.

Neither can we say that I merely know that my car is *probably* parked on Not Utterly Safe St. without rendering many of our quotidian knowledge ascriptions false. Although a belief that probably *p* can be described simply (truly or at least *acceptably* by normal pragmatic standards) as a belief that *p*, as we noted in section 2.3, it is false *and* pragmatically unacceptable to describe knowledge that probably *p* simply as knowledge that *p*, as we also noted. And yet we do say that we know where our cars are parked.

16. A historically important alleged counterexample to closure is in Dretske 1971, which predates Nozick. I know that that is a zebra I see before me in the zoo. I also know that if it is a zebra, then it is not a painted mule. But I do not know that it is not a painted mule (I have done nothing in particular to rule out that possibility or numerous others that are inconsistent with there actually being a zebra before me). This example is more quotidian than the skeptical cases and less quotidian than the car theft cases. There is, I suggest, one respect in which such examples are more like the skeptical cases than the car theft cases. Just as it is odd to say that although we

do not know that we are not brains in vats, we know that we are *probably* not brains in vats, it is equally odd to say that I do not know that there is a painted mule before me, but I know that there *probably* isn't. In both cases, there do not seem to be any grounds for restricting our knowledge to the probabilistic claim but no further: how do we know *just* that, we want to ask? There is no puzzle in saying that we know that the car probably has not been stolen; the grounds for that knowledge claim are thoroughly quotidian.

Dretske's case is also, I think, much less persuasive than the skeptical and car theft cases. I know that zoos do not contain mules painted to look like zebras, so I do know that it is not a painted mule before me. If a very few bogus zoos came into existence, and I was not in one of them, nor was there any real chance that I might have been, it is still plausible that I know that it is not a painted mule before me; even if there is a land of fake barns, if I am nowhere near it when I look at my barn, then I know not just that it is a barn before me but also (at least upon minimal reflection after considering the proposition) that it is not a fake barn. If bogus zoos were legion, then I would not know that it is a zebra before me even if it were. In any case, I do not think that Dretske's cases raise any important issues that the other two classes of counterexamples to closure (and, perhaps, the land of fake barns) do not raise. As with Nozick, Dretske offers a definition of knowledge that has as a consequence that I know that it is a zebra but I do not know that it is not a painted mule despite knowing that if it is a zebra, then it is not a painted mule.

17. I am not proposing the construction of a logic of good inference, even a logic of good *deductive* inference, to supplement classical deductive logic. (However, an AI researcher might very well propose such a thing.)

18. Since inferences on my conception are psychological acts performed by particular individuals, the skeletal arguments at the beginning of this section merely represent hypothetical inferences in enough detail to discuss all actual inferences of a certain class. A difference between Feldman's arguments and my inferences is that he relativizes the goodness of an argument to a person at a time and my inferences are essentially attached to a person at a time, so such relativization would be redundant. (I am not claiming that this is an advantage of my terminology—it is fundamentally a merely terminological issue.) Our aim is the same. I need to acknowledge the fact that whether an inference is good depends on the inferrer's background knowledge since whether he knows the conclusion by inferring it from the premises often depends on what he knows that is not explicitly entertained while he engages in his inference. Feldman needs to acknowledge the corresponding point that whether a person is justified in believing the conclusion of an argument also depends on what he knows that does not figure explicitly in any premise of the argument.

One could relativize one's notion of a good argument more explicitly than Feldman does; rather than relativizing it to persons at times, one could relativize it to the background knowledge, itself explicitly represented in individually expressed propositions, that *could* be possessed by a person at a time. One would thereby have a more general notion of good argument than Feldman or I have. Since an argument can be good for a person on Feldman's view even if the person does not actually believe its conclusion, my conception of inference is the most parochial of the three alternatives. If one has hopes that some kind of formalization of inductive inference will enable one to demonstrate and express precisely substantive results about inductive inference (as, for example, Bayesians do), then one will likely favor the more explicit and general way of representing inference to my own. I have no such aim and no such hope since, as stated above, a *general* explanation of how one can know a conclusion on the basis of knowledge of the premises of an inference is unlikely, and a formalization of inductive inference will, I suggest, serve little purpose unless it serves a goal that is dangerously close to the goal of giving such an explanation. I will return to this issue at the end of the next section.

19. That is, the conditional probability of the conclusion on the conjunction of the premises (perhaps conjoined with background knowledge, on which more below) has such a value.

20. If one adopts Williamson's view of the relation between probability and knowledge together with my view of good inference, the relationship between probability and good inference is simple, but not theoretically interesting.

21. Williamson's identification of evidence with knowledge, on which more below, is perhaps a contemporary elaboration of the traditional idea that one's evidence consists of all and only certainties, although an identification of knowledge and certainty is, of course, quite a break with tradition, at least if we take it as relatively unproblematic that we know much of what we pretheoretically regard ourselves as knowing.

22. Of course, one might not know just *what* one's evidence is evidence for. People in premodern times presumably had quite a lot of evidence for modern scientific theories; they simply did not realize what it was *for*.

23. As does Williamson's parallel account of evidence *simpliciter,* described immediately below.

24. I will often depart from this practice in the discussion of Achinstein's examples below since he is a propositionalist about evidence, and the discussion will be made clearer by sticking to his practice a lot of the time.

25. Although my definition of the evidence-for relation is based on my definition of good inference, I took premises to be propositions as opposed to knowledge of propositions, and I am taking evidence to be the latter. Once again, this is merely a terminological decision; little hangs on it. All things considered, I find that a uniform decision on the ontological category to which premises and evidence should belong makes matters more confusing, not less. If the reader disagrees, I apologize.

26. This conception of evidence is broadly, but not precisely, coextensive with the counterfactual that if *I* were to infer *h* from *e*, then he would know that *h*. The exceptions are typical of attempts at counterfactual definition. Perhaps *I* lacks the background knowledge to know *h* by inference from *e*, although others have such knowledge and could make the good inference, but *I* is sufficiently epistemically responsible that if he were to infer *h* from *e*, he would have such background knowledge. (This is arguably a "backtracking" counterfactual in Lewis's sense [Lewis 1973], and so if we required the counterfactuals in our definition not to be backtracking (as is the orthodox use of a counterfactual in any case), we might be able to avoid the problem.) Still, *e* is not actually evidence that *h* for *I* since he does not actually have such background knowledge.

It might not help to build a reference to actual possession of appropriate background knowledge into a counterfactual definition since *I*'s situation might be such that if he were to infer *h* from *e*, *h* would be false, although it is in fact true, or perhaps *I* would *die* if he started to make an inference from *e* to *h* before completing the process. In these cases, *e* might actually *be* evidence that *h* for *I*, although he would not know *h* for idiosyncratic reasons were he actually to make the inference from *e* to *h*. Similarly, if *I* were to infer *h* from *e*, his very inference might Gettierize him, leaving him without knowledge that *h* for idiosyncratic reasons. *I* is in a land of real barns, but, anomalously, were he to infer that there is a barn before him from the way things look, all barns, or all the barns but the one before him, would be instantaneously replaced by fakes. (Perhaps a supernatural being has it in for *I* in these limited circumstances.) Nevertheless, that things look a certain way is plausibly evidence that there is a barn before him for *I*.

On the other hand, not much seems to hang on whether such idiosyncratic believers count as having evidence that there is a barn before them. Perhaps we should say that *I* could not know in the relevant sense that there is a barn there on the basis of his knowledge that things look a certain way, and so he does not have evidence that there is a barn there, although there is also a sense in which he *could* know—were his idiosyncrasies removed. I will not take a position on these anomalous cases.

27. It is common to talk of there being *some* evidence for a hypothesis, with the implication that there is *only* some evidence for the hypothesis. Such a statement, I suggest, should be understood as communicating, strictly speaking, that there is evidence that there is at least a chance that the hypothesis is true or something similar (a claim that one can know on the basis of the evidence), but no evidence for a stronger claim—that the hypothesis is categorically true, for example.

28. See section 1.3.3 for why I do not consider this to be what rationality consists in.

29. Similarly, it is perhaps somewhat unintuitive in at least some contexts to say that an established theory (that is, a theory one knows to be true) is evidence for one of its consequences. If I were to adopt Williamson's view that *all* knowledge is evidence, then I would have to say this. (Williamson himself explicitly does not offer any view of

the evidence-for relation, although he discusses related matters in Williamson 2000, ch. 10.) But it is not at all unintuitive to say that a known theory provides a *good reason* for believing one of its consequences. Any extra unintuitiveness attaching to the evidence claim is perhaps mere pragmatics, and pragmatics that has a lot of roots in bad theory.

30. The more specific belief that there is a 95 percent chance that David's symptoms are relieved by noon on Monday will, of course, have to be abandoned since it is no longer justified; a slightly weaker replacement belief would be justified.

31. I do not need weaker probabilistic counterparts that are the *real* hypotheses for which Achinstein's examples that motivate his own view present evidence, as I did with his counterexamples to other views. The categorical claims are quite correct in the relevant hypothetical cases.

32. I will not consider whether Achinstein's third condition *successfully* excludes Gettier cases. His discussion of the condition is too brief to do so profitably.

33. Achinstein's happiness with several concepts of evidence, some of which are more central than others, is no doubt based on a happiness with several concepts of 'good reason to believe', some more externalist, some more internalist. I express my own dissatisfaction with such a view earlier in this book, and it extends to a dissatisfaction with an alleged multitude of concepts of evidence and for the same reasons.

34. For three of his four definitions of evidence, at least; there is a subjective concept of evidence for Achinstein, too, which is merely believed to be "(probably) veridical evidence" (Achinstein 2001, 174) by its possessor.

35. Suppose that a very small number of early copies of a newspaper give the erroneous information that Dewey won the election, but the vast majority correctly report that Truman won, and S_2 sees both versions of the paper while S_1 only sees the correct later edition. Suitably elaborated, we can suppose that S_2 knows everything in the way of background knowledge that S_1 does for an inference that Truman won from the belief that such-and-such an edition of the paper said so. That would be a good inference for S_1, but not for S_2.

36. Perhaps we should add that the logical consequences of e or of e *and* b are also not part of b. I am about to suggest that this propositionalist alternative is unworkable, so the details are not very important.

37. And *false,* unknown unknown beliefs, for that matter, but we can allow the propositionalist a maneuver similar to the one that Achinstein employs in his definition of veridical evidence, holding that the evidence-for relation obtains only if h is true.

38. Of course, I doubt that knowledge can be *defined* in terms of the function of a faculty as Plantinga claims. Even if the function of a faculty is to give its possessor a certain kind of *knowledge,* and what that consists in cannot be reduced to

nonepistemic concepts in a remotely illuminating manner, that function can depend upon the faculty having a certain kind of history.

39. Again, I do not think these characteristics can provide a satisfactory definition of knowledge in counterfactual (Nozick 1981) or reliabilist terms, but that a large number of particular cases of knowledge partially consist in such facts is a much weaker claim that is quite plausible.

40. Consider the popular view that which counterfactuals are true depends on what happens in the "nearest" possible worlds in which the antecedents obtain (those most similar to the actual world in the relevant sense in which the antecedents obtain) (Lewis 1973). Which worlds are nearest to the actual world depends upon the history of the actual world; the state of the world at a single time is not enough to determine which counterfactuals are true.

References

Achinstein, Peter. 2001. *The Book of Evidence*. Oxford University Press, Oxford.

Adler, Jonathan E. 1994. "Testimony, Trust, and Knowing." *Journal of Philosophy* 91(5): 264–275.

Adler, Jonathan E. 1996. "Transmitting Knowledge." *Noûs* 30(1): 99–111.

Alston, William P. 1985. "Concepts of Epistemic Justification." *Monist* 68: 57–89.

Alston, William P. 1986. "Internalism and Externalism in Epistemology." *Philosophical Topics* 14(1): 185–226.

Alston, William P. 1993. "Epistemic Desiderata." *Philosophy and Phenomenological Research* 53(3): 527–551.

Armstrong, David M. 1968. *A Materialist Theory of Mind*. Routledge, London.

Audi, Robert. 1982. "Believing and Affirming." *Mind* 91: 115–120.

Bonjour, Laurence. 1985. *The Structure of Empirical Knowledge*. Harvard University Press, Cambridge, Mass.

Burge, Tyler. 1993. "Content Preservation." *Philosophical Review* 102(4): 457–488.

Coady, C. A. J. 1992. *Testimony: A Philosophical Study*. Clarendon Press, Oxford.

Cohen, Stewart. 1999. "Contextualism, Scepticism, and the Structure of Reasons." *Philosophical Perspectives* 13: 57–89.

Crimmins, Mark. 1992. "Tacitness and Virtual Beliefs." *Mind and Language* 7(3): 240–263.

DeRose, Keith. 1992. "Contextualism and Knowledge Attributions." *Philosophy and Phenomenological Research* 52: 913–929.

DeRose, Keith. 1995. "Solving the Skeptical Problem." *Philosophical Review* 104: 1–52.

DeRose, Keith. 1996. "Knowledge, Assertion, and Lotteries." *Australasian Journal of Philosophy* 74: 568–580.

Descartes, René. 1996. *Meditations On First Philosophy*. Cambridge University Press, Cambridge.

Dretske, Fred. 1971. "Epistemic Operators." *Journal of Philosophy* 67: 1007–1023.

Dretske, Fred. 1982. "A Cognitive Cul-De-Sac." *Mind* 91(361): 109–111.

Feldman, Richard. 1994. "Good Arguments." In Frederick F. Schmitt (ed.), *Socializing Epistemology*, 155–188. Rowman and Littlefield, Lanham, MD.

Feldman, Richard. 2000. "The Ethics of Belief." *Philosophy and Phenomenological Research* 60: 667–695.

Feldman, Richard. 2001. "Voluntary Belief and Epistemic Evaluation." In Steup 2001b, 77–92.

Feldman, Richard, and Earl Conee. 1985. "Evidentialism." *Philosophical Studies* 48: 15–34.

Field, Hartry. 1978. "Mental Representation." *Erkenntnis* 13: 9–61.

Field, Hartry. 1998. "Epistemological Nonfactualism and the A Prioricity of Logic." *Philosophical Studies* 92: 1–24.

Foley, Richard. 1979. "Justified Inconsistent Beliefs." *American Philosophical Quarterly* 16: 247–257.

Foley, Richard. 1992. "The Epistemology of Belief and the Epistemology of Degrees of Belief." *American Philosophical Quarterly* 29: 111–124.

Foley, Richard. 1993. *Working Without a Net*. Oxford University Press, Oxford.

Fricker, Elizabeth. 1987. "The Epistemology of Testimony." *Proceedings of the Aristotelian Society, Supplementary Volume* 61: 57–83.

Fricker, Elizabeth. 1994. "Against Gullibility." In Matilal and Chakrabarti 1994, 125–161.

Gettier, Edmund. 1963. "Is Justified True Belief Knowledge?" *Analysis* 23: 121–123.

Ginet, Carl. 2001. "Deciding to Believe." In Steup 2001b, 63–76.

Goldman, Alvin. 1976. "Discrimination and Perceptual Knowledge." *Journal of Philosophy* 73: 771–791.

Goldman, Alvin. 1986. *Epistemology and Cognition*. Harvard University Press, Cambridge, Mass.

Goldman, Alvin. 1988. "Strong and Weak Justification." *Philosophical Perspectives* 2: 51–69.

Goldman, Alvin. 1992. *Liasons*. MIT Press, Cambridge, Mass.

Goldman, Alvin. 1999. "Internalism Exposed." *Journal of Philosophy* 96(6): 271–293.

Goodman, Nelson. 1983. *Fact, Fiction, and Forecast*. Harvard University Press, Cambridge, Mass.

Graham, Peter. 2000. "Transferring Knowledge." *Noûs* 34(1): 131–152.

Hardwig, John. 1985. "Epistemic Dependence." *Journal of Philosophy* 82(7): 335–349.

Hardwig, John. 1991. "The Role of Trust in Knowledge." *Journal of Philosophy* 88(12): 693–708.

Harman, Gilbert. 1973. *Thought*. Princeton University Press, Princeton.

Hawthorne, John. 2004. *Knowledge and Lotteries*. Oxford University Press, Oxford.

Heller, Mark. 1999. "The Proper Role for Contextualism in an Anti-Luck Epistemology." *Philosophical Perspectives* 13: 115–130.

Hempel, Carl G. 1945. "Studies in the Logic of Confirmation." *Mind* 54: 1–26, 97–121.

Hunter, Daniel. 1996. "On the Relation Between Categorical and Probabilistic Belief." *Noûs* 30(1): 75–98.

Kornblith, Hilary. 2001. "Epistemic Obligation and the Possibility of Internalism." In Abrol Fairweather and Linda Zagzebski (eds.), *Virtue Epistemology*, 231–248. Oxford University Press, Oxford.

Lackey, Jennifer. 1999. "Testimonial Knowledge and Transmission." *Philosophical Quarterly* 49(197): 471–490.

Lewis, David. 1970. "How to Define Theoretical Terms." *Journal of Philosophy* 67: 427–446.

Lewis, David. 1973. *Counterfactuals*. Blackwell, Oxford.

Lewis, David. 1996. "Elusive Knowledge." *Australasian Journal of Philosophy* 74: 549–567.

Lycan, William G. 1986. "Tacit Belief." In Radu J. Bogdan (ed.), *Belief: Form, Content, and Function*, 61–82. Clarendon Press, Oxford.

Matilal, B. K., and A. Chakrabarti (eds.). 1994. *Knowing From Words*. Kluwer Academic Publishers, Dordrecht, the Netherlands.

Merricks, Trenton. 1995. "Warrant Entails Truth." *Philosophy and Phenomenological Research* 55: 841–857.

Nelkin, Dana K. 2000. "The Lottery Paradox, Knowledge, and Rationality." *Philosophical Review* 109(3): 373–409.

Nozick, Robert. 1981. *Philosophical Explanations*. Harvard University Press, Cambridge, Mass.

Parfit, Derek. 1986. *Reasons and Persons*. Oxford University Press, Oxford.

Plantinga, Alvin. 1993a. *Warrant and Proper Function*. Oxford University Press, Oxford.

Plantinga, Alvin. 1993b. *Warrant: The Current Debate*. Oxford University Press, Oxford.

Plantinga, Alvin. 1997. "Warrant And Accidentally True Belief." *Analysis* 57(2): 140–145.

Putnam, Hilary. 1975. "The Meaning of 'Meaning'." In *Mind, Language, and Reality*, 215–271. Cambridge University Press, Cambridge.

Reid, Thomas. 1970. *An Inquiry into the Human Mind*. University of Chicago Press, Chicago.

Richard, Mark. 1990. *Propositional Attitudes: An Essay on Thoughts and How We Ascribe Them*. Cambridge University Press, Cambridge.

Russell, Bertrand. 1912. *The Problems of Philosophy*. Oxford University Press, Oxford.

Slote, Michael. 1979. "Assertion and Belief." In Jonathan Dancy (ed.), *Papers on Language and Logic*. Keele University Library, Keele.

Sosa, Ernest. 1991a. *Knowledge In Perspective*. Cambridge University Press, Cambridge.

Sosa, Ernest. 1991b. "Reliabilism and Intellectual Virtue." In Sosa 1991a, 131–145.

Sosa, Ernest. 1999. "Skepticism and the Internal/External Divide." In John Greco and Ernest Sosa (eds.), *The Blackwell Guide to Epistemology*, 145–157. Blackwell, Oxford.

Steup, Matthias. 2001a. "Introduction." In Steup 2001b, 3–18.

Steup, Matthias (ed.). 2001b. *Knowledge, Truth, and Duty*. Oxford University Press, Oxford.

Sutton, Jonathan. 2005. "Stick to What You Know." *Noûs* 39(3): 359–396.

Unger, Peter. 1975. *Ignorance: A Case for Scepticism*. Oxford University Press, Oxford.

van Fraassen, Bas. 1989. *Laws and Symmetry*. Oxford University Press, Oxford.

Vogel, Jonathan. 1990. "Are There Counterexamples to the Closure Principle?" In Michael D. Roth and Glenn Ross (eds.), *Doubting: Contemporary Perspectives on Scepticism*, 20–23. Kluwer Academic Publishers, Dordrecht, the Netherlands.

Weiner, Matthew. 2004. "Deductive Closure and the Sorites." Presented at the 2004 Annual Meeting of the Pacific Division of the American Philosophical Association.

Welbourne, Michael. 1979. "The Transmission of Knowledge." *Philosophical Quarterly* 29(114): 1–9.

Welbourne, Michael. 1994. "Testimony, Knowledge, and Belief." In Matilal and Chakrabarti 1994, 297–313.

Williams, Bernard. 1973. *Problems of the Self*. Cambridge University Press, Cambridge.

Williamson, Timothy. 1994. *Vagueness*. Routledge, London.

Williamson, Timothy. 2000. *Knowledge and Its Limits*. Oxford University Press, Oxford.

Wright, Crispin. 1991. "Scepticism and Dreaming: Imploding The Demon." *Mind* 100: 87–116.

Wright, Crispin. 1996. "Response to Commentators." *Philosophy and Phenomenological Research* 56: 911–941.

Zagzebski, Linda Trinkhaus. 1996. *Virtues of the Mind*. Cambridge University Press, Cambridge.

Index